IMAGES OF WAR

ARMOURED WARFARE

ON THE
EASTERN FRONT

IMAGES OF WAR

ARMOURED WARFARE

ON THE

EASTERN FRONT

RARE PHOTOGRAPHS FROM
WARTIME ARCHIVES

ANTHONY TUCKER-JONES

Pen & Sword
MILITARY

First published in Great Britain in 2011 by
PEN & SWORD MILITARY
an imprint of
Pen & Sword Books Ltd,
47 Church Street,
Barnsley,
South Yorkshire.
S70 2AS

A CIP record for this book is available from the British Library.

ISBN 978184 884 2809

Typeset by Chic Media Ltd

Printed and bound by CPI

Pen & Sword Books Ltd incorporates the Imprints of
Pen & Sword Aviation, Pen & Sword Maritime, Pen & Sword Military,
Wharncliffe Local History, Pen & Sword Select, Pen & Sword Military
Classics, Leo Cooper, Remember When, Seaforth Publishing and
Frontline Publishing.

For a complete list of Pen & Sword titles please contact
Pen & Sword Books Limited
47 Church Street, Barnsley, South Yorkshire, S70 2AS, England
E-mail: enquiries@pen-and-sword.co.uk
Website: www.pen-and-sword.co.uk

Contents

Preface

Most military historians have a fascination for contemporary images, which often tell a personal story that is not always immediately available from after the battle intelligence reports, HQ diaries and individual memoirs. They represent a frozen moment in time, contrived or otherwise. Indeed, picture editing is part and parcel of the historian's discipline. When it comes to chronicling the massive tank battles fought in the East there is often a notable disparity in the quality of the two sides' photographic records.

There is a perception that the Second World War is seen purely in terms of black and white; this is not strictly true, though the vast majority of images were black and white, especially on the Eastern Front. In the West images were generally the result of the work of officially sanctioned war photographers, while in the East German soldiers took thousands of unofficial snapshots in the early stages of the war, many of which are of remarkable quality and clarity. Hundreds if not thousands of German soldiers gleefully posed on top of knocked-out Soviet tanks in the summer of 1941. After victories in Poland, France, the Balkans and now Russia they felt invincible and it showed on their faces. Even today there is a thriving market for such photo albums, many of which have been broken up over the years and their contents scattered among photo libraries and private collectors.

Many of the German photographs taken on the Eastern Front exhibit a greater honesty than the official Soviet photographers, who were always under pressure to glorify the Red Army's achievements. This partly explains why there are always more Soviet 'action' shots, though this is partially compensated for by dramatic German newsreel footage accompanied by strident narration. The only down side is that many images taken by individual German soldiers were often given at best only the most perfunctory captions and therein lies the challenge for the historian, who often has to embark on a degree of detective work to explain exactly what it is we are seeing. By the end of the war in the East it was the Soviets who had the monopoly on photographing the battlefield, as German troops were too busy struggling to survive to worry about chronicling their slow and painful defeat. There was no imperative to photograph the panzers when most lay twisted and shattered by powerful Soviet anti-tank guns.

While it is not too difficult to appreciate the vast scale of the tank battles fought on the Eastern Front, it is less easy to grasp the myriad factors that contributed to either victory or defeat. Essentially armoured warfare on the Eastern Front was shaped by geography, technology and numbers, and Soviet factories soon ensured that the Red Army enjoyed numerical superiority. While Byelorussia and Ukraine were on the whole suited to armoured warfare the Pripyat Marshes helped shape the strategic options of the two sides. Much has been made of Russia's many rivers, which ironically did little to protect the Soviet Union from Adolf Hitler's Blitzkrieg, or indeed to impede the Red Army's progress once it had eventually recovered from the initial German onslaught.

In their efforts to counter each other's weapons, especially armour, the German and Soviet armies adopted very different approaches. The victories of 1941 in part lulled the Germans into a false sense of security when it came to tank production and development. Crucially the Germans proved incapable of standardisation, producing a plethora of tanks, assault guns and self-propelled guns. The abandonment of the Panzer Mk III in favour of assault guns, essentially a defensive weapon, soon signalled that Hitler had lost the strategic initiative. Subsequent German heavy tanks proved time-consuming to manufacture, were often unreliable and could not be produced in decisive numbers.

The Soviets, on the other hand, were not slow to learn from the disasters of 1941, First, they rescued their vital tank factories, and to buy time threw into combat the remains of their existing tank fleet; then they discarded those tank designs that had been found wanting and concentrated on fine-tuning the T-34. Once this tank had been up-gunned and could be produced in decisive numbers, the fighting largely became attritional. Also Soviet tank designers prudently opted to keep the T-34 simple, robust and easy to build and repair. German tactical and even strategic abilities ultimately counted for little against superior Soviet numbers. Adapting the Blitzkrieg style to their own ends, the Red Army became a metal steamroller that simply pulverised Hitler's panzers.

Photograph Sources

This book would not have been possible without the able assistance of the Stavka Photo Library run by Eastern Front expert Nik Cornish, who has written and illustrated a number of Eastern Front titles in this Images of War series, and the private Eastern Front collection of Canadian Scott Pick. These two men have built up collections that are unrivalled outside of museum holdings. Both have a fascinating range of images taken by both official war photographers and individual soldiers, depicting the many aspects of the conflict between Nazi Germany and Soviet Russia, many of them previously unpublished.

In particular, many of the Scott Pick images are seeing the public light of day for the very first time and I offer thanks to him for agreeing to share them with us. His collection contains many fine 'trophy' shots, such as those taken by individual German soldiers of their comrades standing triumphantly on top of disabled Soviet armour in the early stages of the war. As readers will see, the clarity of these is outstanding and each tells its own particular and sometimes gruesome story.

Lastly I have also drawn some images from my own collection, which derives from a variety of sources, and again many of these are being published for the very first time. Picture editing is a very subjective art and the final selection in this book rests with me – I hope that readers enjoy them.

Photo Credits

The following photographs are courtesy of the Museum of the Armed Forces, Moscow, via Nik Cornish: AO36, AO38, AO41, AO42, AO44, AO45, AO46, AO47, AO48, AO120, AO146, AO153, B84, B89, BA3, BA24, BA51, BA52, BA55, K10, K14, K180, K184, K191, K194 and T49.

The following are from the Russian State Documentary Film and Photo Archive (RGAKFD) in Krasnogorsk, again via Nik Cornish: A44, A46, B19, B21, B25, B26, BA18, BA28, BA211, K5, K6, K9, K17, K22, K25, K78, K174, K175 and L32.

All images with a WH reference number and RA 31 are credited to Nik Cornish at Stavka.

Introduction

The Road to Barbarossa

Along the boulevards and in the parks of the Soviet Union's major cities in the summer of 1941 talk among Soviet citizens was of war. Much of Europe was either allied to Adolf Hitler, subjugated by him or in open conflict. With the Nazis now so firmly ensconced in western Poland, the question on everyone's lips was what were Hitler's intentions towards Mother Russia? The Soviet Union's cultural elite, its artists, writers and filmmakers, had been harnessed to support Stalin's propaganda: Berlin was Moscow's friend. Nevertheless, while the Soviet press was heavily censored, there was no hiding what the Nazis had been up to in western Europe, Scandinavia and the Balkans. Hitler's incredibly successful panzer-led Blitzkrieg could not be easily ignored.

From the old men playing chess on park benches to the babushkas in the bustling markets, talk was never very far from war. Sons had been fighting in the Far East and in Finland or were on liberation duties in the Baltic States. For the average Russian, Byelorussian and Ukrainian, it was hard to believe that Nazi Germany would be so foolish as to invade the well-armed Soviet Union. Besides, Stalin and his coterie of sycophants sitting in the Kremlin had made sure that Mother Russia was safe from attack by creating a buffer zone stretching through southern Finland, the Baltic States and eastern Poland. The Red Army's doctrine of forward defence was assured – or so the public thought. If there were to be war, Poland would be where the panzers were stopped.

The Soviet public's perception of the Red Army was that it was a massive, well-equipped force that the Nazis would be mad to attack. The Soviet press had been full of its heroic exploits in Spain, Mongolia and in neighbouring Finland. Only the upper echelons of the Soviet leadership knew the truth: that despite all the impressive window-dressing in the shape of military hardware, the Red Army was hardly a competent fighting force. There can be no denying that in 1941 it was far from a modern force; its treatment at the hands of Stalin and its performance on the battlefield in recent years were to lull Hitler into a false sense of security with disastrous results.

The German–Soviet Rapallo Treaty helped Germany sidestep the military restrictions of the Versailles Treaty, which had limited its armed forces to 100,000 men, banned conscription, and restricted the production of tanks, fighter planes and submarines. In return for diplomatic recognition, the Soviet government granted Germany access to much-needed Russian raw materials and food. The fledgling Red Army also granted the Germans training facilities where they could try out prohibited equipment. A tank school was set up at Kazan, a flying school at Lipetsk and a chemical warfare centre near Volsk, sowing the seeds for the panzerwaffe and Luftwaffe. Future field generals who attended these training schools included Heinz Guderian, father of Germany's panzerwaffe.

This relationship stopped in 1933 when Hitler came to power. Within two years, he had effectively torn up the Versailles Treaty, reintroducing conscription, building panzers and other military hardware and reoccupying the demilitarised Rhineland. This heralded his policy of conquest through military creep. Britain and France stood by and did nothing, and Hitler took this as a sign of weakness and accelerated his policy of rapid military expansion throughout Europe.

In the meantime Stalin was not blind to Hitler's stated aim of carving out living space or Lebensraum in the east, and turned to Britain and France for help. As far as they were concerned Stalin was worse than Hitler, who seemed to be working wonders with the German economy; besides the Soviets made no secret of their desire to regain lost imperial possessions. Stalin watched as Hitler annexed Austria and partitioned Czechoslovakia with impunity. Not invited to the Munich Conference, which let Hitler have his way with Czechoslovakia, Stalin was left with little option but to deal directly with the Nazis.

The Western Allies were completely taken by surprise when, on 21 August 1939, the Soviet news agency Tass announced that Joachim von Ribbentrop, Hitler's foreign minister, was flying to Moscow to sign a non-aggression pact with Stalin. This pact, signed four days later, granted Hitler a free hand to invade Poland the following month. This action finally brought Britain and France into conflict with Hitler.

What nobody knew at the time was that the pact included a secret agreement for the 'Fourth Partition'. Signed just two days after the pact, this called for the partition of Poland between Germany and the Soviet Union. Estonia, Finland, Latvia and Lithuania were also recognised as being in the Soviet sphere. Stalin was intent on regaining the tiny Baltic states as well as the Karelian Isthmus from Finland (to protect Leningrad), in an attempt to safeguard his western borders.

At dawn on 1 September 1939 Hitler's Wehrmacht began the onslaught on Poland, a nation that both Britain and France had pledged to support in the event of a threat to her independence or territorial integrity. Sixteen days later the Red Army rolled into eastern Poland along an 800-mile front to link up with the victorious Wehrmacht, which in the preceding weeks had systematically crushed the

Polish Army. Just ten days later Warsaw surrendered and by 6 October 1939 the fighting was over.

Two weeks after moving into Poland, Stalin ordered the Finns to hand over the Karelian Isthmus; when they refused, once more the Red Army rolled in only to receive an unexpected bloody nose. Alarmingly, Britain and France almost found themselves at war with Germany and the Soviet Union as they were poised to help the beleaguered Finns; however, after dogged resistance the Finns gave in to Stalin's demands in March 1940.

Stalin now felt secure in the belief that Hitler would never dare fight a two-front war, but in just three months, from April to June 1940, the Wehrmacht overran Denmark, Norway, Luxembourg, Belgium, the Netherlands and France, leaving Britain under threat of invasion. It soon became apparent that major German military preparations in German-occupied Poland, East Prussia, Romania and Finland all indicated Hitler was planning to strike the Soviet Union, but Hitler reassured Stalin that the troop movements eastwards were simply designed to mislead Churchill into lowering his guard. Stalin took him at his word.

Soviet Defence Minister Marshal Semyon Konstantinovich Timoshenko and Chief of the General Staff General Georgi Zhukov were not convinced, and in May 1941 sought Stalin's permission for a pre-emptive attack, but the latter did not want to provoke Hitler's battle-hardened Wehrmacht. Meanwhile Hitler moved into the Balkans, securing his southern flank ready to strike east. There can be no denying that the war that followed on the Eastern Front was foremost a tank war. Indeed, the Soviet Union witnessed some of the biggest and bloodiest tank battles the world has ever seen.

Chapter One

Stalin's Armoured Fist

In the summer of 1941 Joseph Stalin had a huge tank force of 20,000 vehicles with which to protect the Soviet Union from the menace of Adolf Hitler. Zhukov had been instructed to prepare State Defence Plan 1941; based on the premise that Red Army operations would be in response to a Nazi attack, the idea was to take the war to the enemy in an offensive rather than defensive manner. The overall strength of Stalin's armed forces in early 1941 was almost 5 million men, 2.6 million of them in the west, 1.8 million in the Far East, and the rest being redeployed or under training.

Of the Red Army's 303 divisions (of which 88 were still in the process of formation), 237 were in the west. However, Stalin's reluctance to mobilise for war and the logistics involved meant that when war broke out, only 171 divisions were actually in the field, deployed in three operational belts comprising 57, 52 and 62 divisions, along with his 20 mechanised corps supported by about 1,800 heavy and medium tanks and thousands of light tanks. This meant that only a third of the divisions were actually in the first defensive echelon and the tanks were dispersed where they could be easily destroyed piecemeal by Hitler's panzers.

To Stalin's way of thinking, if Hitler did invade he would undoubtedly go for the raw materials of Ukraine, and as a result most of the Red Army's mechanised corps were with Colonel General M.P. Kirponos's South Western Front. This had a large number of armoured units, notably six mechanised corps plus two reserve corps. In Lvov (Lemberg), formerly in eastern Poland but now part of Ukraine, was the 4th Mechanised Corps with General Andrei Vlasov. He did not know it, but he was to play a very infamous role in Hitler's war in the East. His command included the 32nd Tank Division equipped with 300 lumbering KV-1 tanks. When the time came, elements of this division would offer effective if short-lived opposition to the panzers. Further east, stationed in the Ukrainian capital Kiev, was General K.K. Rokossovsky's 9th Mechanised Corps.

The infantry constituted 75 per cent of the line divisions, and the Soviets could muster four types of rifle division, totalling 178 basic rifle divisions, 31 motor rifle divisions (in theory assigned to the mechanised corps), 18 mountain rifle divisions and 2 independent rifle divisions. Despite being called motor rifle troops, the reality was that many ended up riding on the outside of the tanks. Following the disastrous performance of the Red Army in Finland, the rifle division was reorganised, to consist of three infantry and two artillery regiments plus anti-tank and anti-aircraft support. As all the armour went to the new mechanised corps, each rifle division was left with only 16 light tanks – a fatal weakness by anyone's reckoning.

It was only at the last minute that Stalin and Stavka, the Soviet high command, acquiesced in the creation of these fully fledged mechanised corps grouping the tank and motorised divisions, but by then it was too late. This process only began in March 1941 and of the proposed 20 mechanised corps (each with one tank and two motorised infantry divisions), fewer than half had been equipped by June. For example, on the eve of war, while the 12th Mechanised Corps was able to muster 84 per cent of its tanks, the 3rd Mechanised Corps could only manage 55 per cent. The latter's armour comprised mostly inadequate T-26s, there were a few T-34s and just two new KV-1s. The 7th Mechanised Corps had none of its authorised 420 T-34s and just 40 of its 120 KVs. Clearly this was a recipe for disaster.

The key armoured formation in the south, Rokossovsky's 9th Mechanised Corps, defending the Kiev Special Military District (South West Front from the outbreak of hostilities) was mechanised only in name. Rokossovsky only had a third of his tanks and they were obsolete, with worn-out engines; his motorised infantry lacked even horses and carts. Soviet mechanics must have despaired at trying to maintain the vehicles in their charge. When the time came, Rokossovsky worked miracles and he proved to be exactly the type of general his country needed in its hour of desperation. In the meantime these new formations were on the whole inadequately led, equipped and trained.

To add to the Red Army's difficulties, after moving into eastern Poland it had abandoned and stripped most of the pre-1939 Soviet-Polish frontier defences. This required the construction of new defences in the western areas of the Special Military Districts. This left those Soviet forces in eastern Poland very vulnerable to attack.

Barring the way to Minsk and Moscow was General D.G. Pavlov's Western Special Military District or West Front. His command also comprised just six of the 20 mechanised corps, with a total of 12 tank divisions and six supporting motorised divisions. He was in the unenviable position of holding the Bialystok salient, trapped between East Prussia and German-occupied Poland. There is a suspicion that Stalin and Zhukov considered Pavlov's command something of a sacrificial lamb and that it was the Reserve Front's job to hold Hitler at the old frontier. Certainly by June 1941 the West Front was far from up to strength.

In the Kremlin General Ia N. Fedorenko noted that there were 'too few modern tanks and that a number of tanks which were standard equipment in the Red Army were already obsolete'. He concluded that no time should be lost in increasing production of the new T-34 and KV tanks and that funding should be redirected to this end. Marshal G.I. Kulik, who favoured cavalry and artillery, was dismissive, claiming that the balance was right. After that no one spoke further on the issue. On the very eve of the war the chance to shake up their mechanised forces was lost.

Hitler's Wehrmacht had perfected its 'lightning war' tactics in western Europe, Scandinavia and the Balkans. In the face of the Nazis' tried and tested Blitzkrieg tactics, combining armour with motorised infantry, supported by air and artillery strikes, the outcome was inevitable. Hitler had at most 153 divisions, including reserves, available for operations on the Eastern Front by 22 June 1941; Stalin, though ill-prepared, had almost double that number. In total Hitler could muster about 3 million men; Stalin had 4½ million at his disposal.

Geographically, for Hitler there was the problem of the Soviet front itself, which funnelled out from 1,300 miles to 2,500 miles. These logistical problems were compounded by his lack of reserves; his Replacement Army had less than half a million men, sufficient only for replacements during the intended brief summer campaign. Hitler only had three months' reserves of petrol and one month's of diesel. He was gambling on gaining a quick victory thanks to his panzers. Nor did Hitler seem inclined to consider the long-term value or reliability of his East European Axis allies. Equally worrying was the fact that the superiority of the panzers was not that marked, although General Heinz Guderian believed at the beginning of the campaign that the technical superiority of the German tanks would cancel out the Soviets' massive numerical advantage.

Nonetheless in the spring of 1941 a Soviet Commission's comments on seeing the panzers led German ordnance officials to conclude, 'It seems that the Russians must already possess better and heavier tanks than we do.' The German military really should have come to this conclusion after the Spanish Civil War. It was evident then that Soviet tank design was accelerating and the Soviet T-34 tank was about to make its appearance; it would prove equal to any existing German armour. This design and Soviet industrial might would be Hitler's ultimate undoing.

In the 1930s much of the Red Army's armour comprised the BT (*Bystrokhodnii*) fast tank; the BT-5 (in fact a copy of the US Christie M-1931) is identifiable by its cylindrical turret housing a 45mm gun. The BT was unusual in that it could run on roads at high speeds off its tracks; with a crew of three and a weight of 11.5 tons it could manage 70mph. However, it was time-consuming taking the tracks off and in a country lacking paved roads was not a great asset. (*Author's Collection*)

At the time of Hitler's invasion the bulk of the Soviet fast tanks consisted of the BT-5's up-armoured successor the BT-7, seen here with the newer conical turret, which went into production in 1935 and was known as *Betka* ('Beetle') by its crews. Most of the BT-2/5/7s still in service were replaced by the T-34 within a year of the invasion. (*Scott Pick Collection*)

The single-turret T-26B light tank appeared in 1933 (the earlier T-26 had twin turrets) and was armed with a 45mm or 37mm gun. Its weight, though, rose by a ton to 9 tons, reducing its road speed to 18mph. This low speed and poor mobility compared to the BT-5 resulted in production being abandoned in the mid-1930s. (*Scott Pick Collection*)

Nonetheless, the T-26, developed from the British Vickers 6-ton tank, is considered one of the best designs of the 1930s. Around 11,000 were built, with over 20 variants, making it the most numerous tank at the time of Operation Barbarossa. While it could not cope with the Panzer III or IV, it remained in service until 1944, taking part in the battles for Moscow, Stalingrad and Leningrad. (*Scott Pick Collection*)

While Soviet medium tank designs were initially slow off the mark, the cumbersome-looking T-28 was in production by 1932; it was fitted with three turrets, one mounting a 45mm gun and the other two machine guns. One of the world's very first medium tanks, and intended for an infantry support role, the Red Army had 400 at the time of Hitler's invasion. (*Author's Collection*)

The massive T-35 heavy tank weighed in at 45 tons; it appeared a year after the T-28 and was a similar beast, but only about 60 were ever built. Although only produced in limited numbers, it was regularly photographed by bemused German troops because of its size. Before the war T-35s served in Moscow with the 5th Separate Heavy Tank Brigade performing parade duties from 1935 to 1940. (*Scott Pick Collection*)

The new T-34/76 medium tank first came off the Kharkov Komintern Factory production line in January 1940. The Model 1940 (T-34/76A) is immediately recognisable by the low-slung barrel of the L-11 76.2mm anti-tank gun below a distinctive bulge in the mantlet (housing the recoil mechanism). It also has a very large, single turret hatch, which was heavy and difficult to open. Russian veterans condemned this type and nicknamed it *pirozhok* ('pie') because of its characteristic shape. This tank went into mass production in June and by the end of the year just 115 had been built. (*Scott Pick Collection*)

The subsequent Model 1941 (T-34/76B) had heavier armour and was armed with the superior F-34 76.2mm gun mounted higher in the mantlet, but it still had the single hatch. Subsequent models incorporated two smaller, circular turret hatches. This particular one is under scrutiny by German mechanics; the purpose of the bow saw is unclear. (*Scott Pick Collection*)

From January 1939 to June 1941 the Red Army received over 7,000 new tanks, but the plants managed to put out only 1,861 KV heavy tanks and T-34 medium tanks before the outbreak of war, which was clearly insufficient. This is the KV-2 armed with a 152mm howitzer. (*Scott Pick Collection*)

The T-34/76 appeared in a number of variants largely identified by their year of production, i.e. Model 1940 (A), 1941 (B), 1942 (C and D), 1943 (E and F) T-34, which were all armed with the 76.2mm gun, followed by the up-gunned T-34/85 and T-44 with the 85mm gun. Russian tankers had little interest in such nuances. The cast turret (as opposed to rolled plate) makes this a late Model 1941 or an early Model 1942. (*Scott Pick Collection*)

A notable difference in the appearance of the T-34 occurred with the T-34/76D manufactured from late 1942. This was fitted with a hexagonal turret that did away with the rear overhang on earlier models, which acted as a shell trap and was a tempting target for German Teller anti-tank mines. Also the new turret was slightly larger, offering the crew extra space. (*Author's Collection*)

The Red Army had thousands of light tanks, including the amphibious T-37/38 and T-40 (seen here). The latter came into service in early 1941. If they had been restricted to reconnaissance roles as intended, they could have played a useful role against the Nazi invasion, but instead Soviet commanders used them as regular tanks and wasted them. (*A44*)

Some 1,200 tiny two-man T-37 light amphibious tanks were built between 1933 and 1936. These replaced the T-27 tankette and served with the Red Army tank, mechanised and cavalry units in a reconnaissance role until 1942. (*Author's Collection*)

This photograph showing a column of whitewashed BA-20 armoured cars escorting a convoy of lorries through a forest was issued by the Soviet Ministry of Information. In the late 1930s this became the most popular and numerous type of armoured car in service with the Red Army. (*Author's Collection*)

Notably the BA-20 ZhD variant could be fitted with railway wheels and a number of examples were reused by the Germans to help protect the Soviet rail network from partisans. The spare wheel spigot at the rear acted as a rail tow link so that the vehicle could be towed by a train to act as rear guard with its 7.62mm machine gun. (*Scott Pick Collection*)

The BA-10 was the only heavy armoured car employed by the Red Army during the Second World War (having superseded the BA-27 and BA-6); it was armed with the ubiquitous 45mm gun and around 1,400 were built. BA-10s saw extensive action during the 'Great Patriotic War' and large numbers were pressed into service by the Finnish and German armies. The BA-10M, of which 331 were built, is distinguishable from the BA-10 by the external fuel tanks mounted over the rear wheels. (*Author's Collection*)

Soviet armoured car development was slow and only one new model, known as the BA-64, went into production after the German invasion in late 1941. The BA-64B was fitted with a one-man turret and appeared two years later. (B25)

The T-20 Komsomolets armoured artillery tractor was designed in 1936 at the Ordzhonikidze Moscow Plant no. 37. They were also built at the STZ and GAZ factories during the period 1937–1941. It was designed to tow light support weapons such as the 45mm anti-tank gun and the 120mm heavy mortar. In response to the German invasion, the chassis was used to create the ZiS-30 self-propelled anti-tank gun using the ZIS-2 57mm gun, though only about 100 were produced. (*Author's Collection*)

The T-20 was unsuitable as a weapons or troop carrier. It had an armoured, enclosed compartment at the front for the driver and machine-gunner (in this instance it has done the gunner no good), but the six seats on the back were highly exposed. Nonetheless T-20s were used offensively with predictably fatal results. (*Scott Pick Collection*)

The standard Soviet field guns were the 76.2mm M1936 and M1939, but after the experiences of the German invasion, the Soviets took the view that any gun capable of direct fire should also be used in an anti-tank role. This resulted in the M1942, which was regularly employed in an anti-tank role and was produced in greater numbers than any other artillery piece during the Second World War. (*K194*)

The Soviet M1939 85mm anti-aircraft gun was also issued with anti-tank ammunition and successfully adapted to fit the KV and T-34. Like all Red Army designs, it offered few frills and was very functional. (T49)

The key man-portable anti-tank weapons were the PTRD 1941 anti-tank rifle (seen here) and the PTRS that was developed at the same time. The PTRD proved far more robust in the field and was lighter. (T53)

Chapter Two

Hitler's Axis Armour

Hitler gathered 20 panzer divisions for the invasion of the Soviet Union, codenamed Barbarossa. By 1938 he had raised just five, which had to rely on the inadequately armed Panzer Mk I and II, as deliveries of the newer Panzer III and IV were frustratingly slow. Remarkably two years later he had over 3,300 panzers, a force that had been created from a standing start. However, just 629 of them were Mk III and IV, plus 371 captured Czech PzKpfw 35(t) and 38(t). Even after this absorption of Czechoslovakia's tank force Hitler's panzers were not as strong as he had hoped, although this did not stop him from defeating the Polish and French armies with ease.

After the battle for France Hitler, infatuated by the triumph of the Blitzkrieg, moved to double the number of panzer divisions. This was achieved by halving the number of tanks on the existing divisional establishment. This was not a popular move as it greatly weakened the striking power of a given panzer division. He also sought to double his motorised infantry divisions, adding yet further strain on German industry. In the run-up to Barbarossa the panzer divisions were given an established strength of two or three tank battalions providing 150–202 panzers per division – though in reality they could usually only each field on average 135 operational tanks. The first panzer divisions had originally consisted of four tank battalions.

By the spring of 1941 the Czech armour comprised 25 per cent of Hitler's tank force. For his attack on Stalin, one panzer division was partly equipped with the 35(t), while six others were armed with the 38(t). The 18th Panzer Division found itself issued with captured French tanks. Subsequent attempts to supply French armour to other panzer divisions for operations on the Eastern Front were declined. While the Czech tanks were capable of taking on the various Russian light tanks, such as the T-26, T-37, T-40 and T-60, up against anything heavier they were in trouble. Although reasonably armoured at the front, the 37mm anti-tank gun was simply not capable of taking on the Russian T-34/76 armed with a 76.2mm gun or the similarly armed KV-1. To compound matters, moves to upgrade the Panzer III's armament from 37mm to 50mm had not run smoothly. Hitler discovered in April 1941 that the Ordnance Office had fitted the L/42 50mm instead of the L/60 50mm high-velocity gun that he had ordered.

While events in Russia would soon show the need for a more powerful anti-tank gun, the L/60, although useful against the British Grant and Valentine tanks in North Africa, could not cope with the frontal armour of the T-34 and KV-1. The L/60-armed Panzer III did not go into production until six months after the invasion of the Soviet Union and it was a year before a variant with the short 75mm gun became available. The Panzer III turret would not accommodate a larger gun and eventually production was turned over to a turretless assault gun. With the benefit of hindsight, attacking the Soviet Union with so few Panzer IVs seems the height of folly.

Despite deploying three army groups, totalling 145 divisions, for the invasion of the Soviet Union, Hitler was reliant on the manpower and armour of his squabbling Axis allies to help protect his southern flank. This was to contribute to his defeat, as they proved to be his Achilles heel. Forces sent by Hungary, Italy, Romania and Slovakia to take part in his crusade against Bolshevism were not mechanised and lacked tanks, anti-tank guns and transport. At the time Hungary was the only Eastern European country with an indigenous tank capability. In the opening stages of the war Hungary provided two motorised brigades and a cavalry brigade equipped with about 150 Toldi light tanks, Italian-supplied L.35 tankettes and Csaba armoured cars for Hitler's invasion of Yugoslavia in April 1941.

By June 1941 the Hungarians had just 189 tankettes, light tanks and armoured cars. However, they committed large numbers of troops to Barbarossa, including the Carpathian Group of two brigades and the mobile corps of three brigades. The latter had to seize civilian transport to supplement its obsolete armour. At the time of the invasion Romania had almost 300 largely useless tanks organised into two regiments, including 126 Czech LT-35s. The Romanian 1st Armoured Regiment was the first Romanian unit to take part in the invasion of the USSR.

To this day the role Bulgaria's panzers played is little understood. While it is widely known that the Hungarians and Romanians fought on the Eastern Front alongside the Germans, it is not generally appreciated that the Bulgarian Army first fought with and then against the Germans in the Balkans. King Boris and his high command were in awe of the panzers' Blitzkrieg into the Balkans and sought with meagre resources to create their own armoured forces. The Bulgarians formed their 1st Armoured Regiment in June 1941 under the watchful eye of German instructors. Hitler probably hoped that the Bulgarian armour would eventually be committed to the crusade against Bolshevism in the east. In the event it ended up fighting Bulgarian and Yugoslav partisans and the German army. While Bulgaria took part in the destruction of Yugoslavia and Greece, and eventually declared war on Britain and America, King Boris was less keen to cross Stalin; arguing that his army lacked mechanisation, he prudently avoided taking part in Barbarossa.

The Germans discovered during the Spanish Civil War that the Republicans' Soviet-supplied T-26 tanks were far superior to the Panzer Mk I, which first went into production in the mid-1930s. After seeing action in Poland, France, Scandinavia and North Africa, the Mk I was phased out and when Hitler invaded Russia there were only 74 still with the panzer regiments. They were a rare sight on the Eastern Front. (*Scott Pick Collection*)

The Panzer II, built from 1936 to 1942, was armed with a 20mm gun and was used in Russia in a reconnaissance role. It too was phased out of service with the tank regiments in late 1943, when the chassis was turned over to self-propelled gun production – most notably the Wespe. (*Scott Pick Collection*)

A rare PzKpfw II Ausf D und E; the hull and suspension were of a different design from the normal Panzer IIs, easily identifiable by the four road wheels and no return rollers. These were used on the Eastern Front as flame-throwers until 1942, when they were converted into self-propelled guns using captured Soviet 76.2mm anti-tank guns. (*Author's Collection*)

The Panzer Mk III, armed with a 50mm gun, was superior to any Allied armour until 1942. Later F, G and H models were converted to submersible *Tauchpanzers* and took part in the invasion of Russia in the vanguard of the 18th Panzer Division. While it had its shortcomings, the subsequent Mk IV with its short 75mm gun was able to fire armour-piercing, high explosive and smoke shells. (*Scott Pick Collection*)

A StuG III Ausf B assault gun in action; note the spent shell cases by the road wheels discarded by the gunner. It was armed with the same L/24 short 75mm gun as the Panzer IV, and over 300 of these assault guns were produced by the time of the invasion. Six *sturmartillerie* (assault artillery) units took part in Operation Barbarossa. It was intended as an infantry support weapon, but thanks to its low profile it soon proved itself an able tank killer. (*Author's Collection*)

The 37mm Pak 35/36 was the standard German anti-tank gun at the outbreak of the Second World War, and ironically it was sold to the Soviet Union in large numbers prior to 1940. The Soviet Model 1937 45mm anti-tank gun bore a striking resemblance to it (the earlier 37mm Model 1930 was essentially the same design). It could only cope with the panzers at close range and was replaced by the more powerful Model 1942. (*Scott Pick Collection*)

Due to the inadequacy of the Pak 35/36, the 50mm Pak 38 L/60 anti-tank gun designed by Rheinmetall-Borsig was rushed into service, equipping the anti-tank battalions of the German army and Waffen-SS late in 1940. At 1,000 metres it could just about cope with the T-34. This gun was subsequently retrofitted in many PzKpfw III tanks, which had started life with 37mm guns. (*Scott Pick Collection*)

A scaled-up version of the Pak 38, the 75mm Pak 40 entered service in November 1941 and became the German army's standard anti-tank gun for the rest of the war. Its increased weight meant it was sometimes abandoned to the Russian winter – hence the Soviet gun crew. (*Scott Pick Collection*)

The Flak 36 88mm gun could be deployed in a dual anti-aircraft and anti-tank role and saw continuous service on the Eastern Front throughout the war. Initially it helped compensate for the inadequacy of the German army's 37mm and 50mm anti-tank guns. Its weight, however, meant that only large vehicles could move it, and the SdKfz 7 half-track became a common tow vehicle. (*K175*)

The SdKfz 6/7/8/11 family of half-tracks, used to tow the 88mm Flak gun and the sFH 18 150mm howitzer, also became the basis of a number of self-propelled anti-aircraft variants armed with 20mm and 37mm flak guns. (*Author's Collection*)

The very distinctive SdKfz 251 was the principal armoured personnel carrier for panzergrenadiers. This particular variant, the 251/10, was armed with the Pak 35/36 37mm gun to provide platoon leaders with extra firepower. Some were later fitted with L/43 and L/46 75mm guns, giving it an anti-tank role. (*K174*)

Following Hitler's occupation of Czechoslovakia, he acquired the Skoda LT-35 light tank (seen here) and the designs for the CKD LT-38. The former saw action with the German army in Poland and France. For the invasion of Russia the 6th Panzer Division was equipped with 103 LT-35s. (*Author's Collection*)

The Czech-designed LT-38, known as the PzKpfw 38(t) in German service, was a key element of Hitler's panzer force, although it was under-gunned and under-armoured. It lasted little more than just over a year on the Eastern Front. (*Author's Collection*)

After the fall of France large numbers of French tanks were taken into German service. The Hotchkiss H-35/39 was modified with the installation of a wireless set and a change in the cupola and designated the PzKpfw 39-H 735(f). (*Author's Collection*)

The modern Somua S-35, the best French tank in 1940 and perhaps in Europe, also fell into Hitler's hands. The 211th Panzer Battalion, supporting the Finnish army's attacks towards Leningrad, was equipped with S-35s and H-39s. It was the first French-equipped panzer unit to see action in Russia from the very first day of the invasion. (*Author's Collection*)

A limited number of German panzer divisions, including the 18th, were issued with captured French tanks. Among them were the Renault heavy Char de Bataille B1 Bis armed with a 47mm turret gun and a powerful 75mm hull gun. The Char B was effective against lighter Soviet armour but was no match for their heavier tanks. French armour did not last long in Russia, and by November 1941 the 18th Panzer Division had lost 70 per cent of its French tanks. (*Author's Collection*)

A German liaison officer and his Hungarian colleagues smile for the camera. The Hungarian army eventually provided two armoured divisions for the Eastern Front equipped with Toldi light tanks and Turan medium tanks, as well as Nimrod and Zrinyi self-propelled guns. They were also supplied with some German armour. (*Author's Collection*)

The Hungarian-built Toldi light tank was based on the Swedish Landsverk L60 and was no match for Soviet armour. In the opening stages of the war Hungary's mechanised forces comprised two motorised brigades and a cavalry brigade equipped with obsolete tankettes, light tanks and armoured cars. (*Author's Collection*)

Motorised Slovak infantry on parade. Initially Slovakia provided two infantry divisions to support Hitler's Army Group South. These were later replaced by the Slovak Mobile Division, which included a solitary Skoda tank company. (*Author's Collection*)

The Hungarian Turan medium tank, based on the Czech LT-35, was obsolete before it even went into production in 1941. The Turan I was armed with a 40mm gun, while the subsequent Turan II had a 75mm gun; in total about 500 of both types were built. (*Author's Collection*)

Only 60 Hungarian Zrinyi self-propelled howitzers were built during 1943 and 1944, and they had no impact on the war. (AO38)

This Romanian cavalryman, and the horse-drawn transport behind, illustrates the extent of the Romanian army's mechanisation. Its 1st Armoured Regiment, equipped with LT-35s, was the only tank unit to take part in the invasion of the USSR. Romania's only other armoured regiment, with Renault R-35s, was not committed for lack of spares. (Author's Collection)

Chapter Three

Barbarossa – The Red Army Smashed

On 22 June 1941 Hitler threw 3,200 panzers at Stalin's enormous tank force of some 20,000 vehicles; in his favour, only about 60 per cent of them were serviceable and most were obsolete, dating from the 1930s. The Germans were able to knock out huge numbers of Soviet tanks because they were poorly deployed and vulnerable, often cooking the crews, despite the Red Army having learned its lesson the hard way fighting the Japanese and Finns in 1939.

Within just three weeks Stalin lost 2 million men, 3,500 tanks and 6,000 aircraft to Hitler's unrelenting Blitzkrieg. Within five months Hitler had destroyed or captured 17,000 tanks for the loss of 2,700 panzers, and had reached the very gates of Moscow. Soviet losses were such that they could muster only 780 tanks for the defence of Moscow. For a while the decimated Red Army suffered an acute shortage of tanks, guns and aircraft.

Hitler's titanic assault on Stalin began at 03.15am on Sunday 22 June 1941, heralded by air attacks on 66 frontier airfields; the result was that the Red Air Force was swiftly taken out of the equation. Some 550 bombers and 480 fighters were involved in the raids. Hitler's strike force also included an additional 300 Stuka dive-bombers. A hail of fragmentation bombs fell on runways, taxiing strips and hangars. Soviet aircraft were either destroyed on the ground or shot out of the air as they rose to meet the Luftwaffe. They lost 1,200 aircraft by noon.

This left the Red Army at the mercy of the marauding Luftwaffe. Soviet troop concentrations were bombed and strafed as they sought to mass in order to conduct counter-attacks. On the day of the invasion German aircraft bombing Lvov airport also struck the barracks of Vlasov's 32nd Tank Division.

Hitler's forces rolled relentlessly across eastern Poland, evicting the Red Army, and into Byelorussia. Army Group North thrust towards Leningrad, Army Group Centre headed for Moscow and Army Group South cut deep into Ukraine. Further south, combined German, Hungarian and Romanian forces drove into the Caucasus, while to the far north the Finns thrust toward Murmansk and down the Karelian

Isthmus as part of the 'Continuation War'. Pre-1939 Soviet gains in both Poland and Finland were soon lost.

General Heinz Guderian's 2nd Panzer Group's key armoured formations comprised three panzer corps, which included five panzer divisions. General H. Hoth's 3rd Panzer Group included two further corps encompassing four panzer divisions. In their path were the Red Army forces of Pavlov's 3rd, 10th and 4th Armies. His attempts at holding the Germans at bay proved futile as the 6th and 11th Mechanised and 6th Cavalry Corps' counter-attacks were crushed and Minsk was encircled. Armoured units trapped in the Minsk pocket included the 20th Mechanised Corps, the 4th and 7th Tank Divisions and the 8th Tank Brigade. Stalin and his generals became obsessed with launching rushed and ill-conceived counter-attacks and rapidly threw away their mechanised corps.

In the south on 22 June General M.P. Kirponos tried to get his harassed 15th and 22nd Mechanised Corps to counter the Germans' flanks. Only a weak element of the 15th's 10th Tank Division was committed, but to little effect, and the panzers penetrated 24 miles to Berestechko. Likewise the 22nd's 215th Motorised and 19th Tank Divisions were unable to prevent the panzers reaching Lutsk. When mustered, the 15th's 10th and 37th Tank Divisions were unable to stop the panzers pushing on another 18 miles.

Likewise Rokossovsky's 9th and General N.V. Feklenko's 19th Mechanised Corps were ordered to counter-attack north of Dubno, while to the south I.I. Karpezo's 15th and D.I. Riabyshev's 8th Mechanised Corps were also to attack. Unfortunately Zhukov and Kirponos' orders led to Vlasov's 4th Mechanised Corps being dispersed, preventing its forces from supporting the 8th Mechanised Corps.

The counter-attack was launched on 26 June, resulting in a battle involving over 2,000 tanks. During the fighting the 8th Mechanised Corps was surrounded and the 15th made little headway. In the north the 19th Corps ran into two panzer divisions and was driven back to Rovno. Rokossovsky conducted his attack on the 27th, only to suffer heavy losses, and was ordered back. While it was overall a failure, this Soviet counter-offensive delayed Hitler for a week and convinced him that he needed to secure Ukraine, which would have ramifications for Army Group Centre's drive on Moscow.

In Byelorussia on 28 June Minsk fell to Army Group Centre; with the liquidation of the Minsk pocket the Germans claimed to have destroyed or captured 4,799 tanks and 9,427 guns and to have taken 341,000 prisoners. The subsequent seizure of Smolensk yielded similar results, as did the massive encirclements at Vyazma and Bryansk. On 30 June Army Group Centre entered Lvov, the 32nd Tank Division having fled the city and gone back to Kiev. Likewise the rest of Vlasov's 4th Mechanised Corps was long gone.

Stavka's other counter-strokes launched the newly arrived 5th and 7th Mechanised Corps at Hoth's 3rd Panzer Group in Byelorussia on 6 July. In five days of fighting near Senno and Lepel they lost 832 of their 2,000 tanks. This left the panzers free to press on towards Smolensk. In a desperate move to restore the situation along the Dnepr Zhukov instructed Timoshenko's Western Front to conduct counter-attacks along its full length. Also on 6 July Timoshenko threw the 6th and 7th Mechanised Corps, with a total of 700 tanks, at the flanks of the German XXXIX Panzer Corps north of Orsha. Lacking air cover, they headed for Senno and came across the 17th and 18th Panzer Divisions. A week later a German breakthrough heralded the encirclement of Smolensk and 300,000 Soviet troops were cut off between the city and Orsha.

During the first 18 days of the war the Soviet Western Front, defending eastern Poland and western Byelorussia, lost more than 417,000 men killed, wounded or missing, as well as 9,427 guns and mortars, more than 4,700 tanks, and 1,797 aircraft.

Crucially, at the end of July 1941 Hitler decided that Army Group Centre would go over to the defensive, and the diversion of part of its forces to support Army Group South's capture of Kiev from the Soviet South Western Front fatally delayed the drive on Moscow. However, at Kiev two-thirds of a million Soviet troops were caught in a pocket the size of Belgium, and for the first and last time the German Army outnumbered the Red Army. All eyes then turned back to Army Group Centre.

Panzer IIIs roll over the border. On 22 June 1941 Hitler's Operation Barbarossa swept through Soviet defences in eastern Poland and into western Russia. He struck Stalin's Red Army on three strategic axes, with Army Group North aiming for Leningrad, Army Group Centre striking for Moscow and Army Group South targeting Kiev. The bulk of the Red Army's armoured forces lay in the path of Army Group Centre. (*Scott Pick Collection*)

Columns of Panzer IIIs and Panzer IIs pushed through Russian villages in the face of little or no opposition. There were seventeen panzer divisions on the border; six had been issued with PzKpfw 38(t) and eleven had PzKpfw IIII. Despite repeated warnings from Stalin's senior generals, Hitler's Blitzkrieg caught the Red Army completely off guard. (*Scott Pick Collection*)

Czech designed and built LT-38 light tanks advancing into Russia; they equipped the 7th, 8th, 12th, 19th, 20th and 22nd Panzer Divisions for Barbarossa. (*Author's Collection/Scott Pick Collection*)

Behind the panzers came the support weapons and infantry. This sequence of photos shows a convoy of captured French Chenillette tracked infantry carriers towing Pak 35/36 anti-tank guns. The two-man crew were only protected by 7mm of armour, their heads enclosed by the distinctive steel domes. After the fall of France Hitler gained 6,000 carriers, many of which were re-employed as the Infanterie Schlepper UE 630(f). (*Author's Collection*)

The harsh reality of the situation in the summer of 1941 was that the masses of BT-5/7 and T-26 were obsolete and could simply not cope with the Panzer Mk III and IV medium tanks or the Sturmgeschütz III assault gun, while the T-28 and heavy tanks like the T-35 and KV-1 were easily outmanoeuvred. This BT-7 seems to have reversed into a river in a desperate bid to escape its attackers, perhaps betraying the inexperience of the crew. (*Scott Pick Collection*)

German troops examine the spoils of war – abandoned BT-7s. Although the Red Army was deployed in depth, it was poorly sited and the Germans swiftly cut through its defences, leaving a trail of death and destruction. In the way of the 2nd and 3rd Panzer Groups lay the Soviet 3rd, 10th and 4th Armies; Hitler's panzers easily brushed aside the 10th, 19th and 37th Tank Divisions. (*Scott Pick Collection*)

The interior of this T-26 provides some fascination for the victors, who may be trying to coax out a very frightened Soviet tanker. (*Scott Pick Collection*)

Some 1,125 T-34 tanks had been produced by June 1941. Although it eventually proved to be the world's best tank, initially there were too few of them and they were often driven by incompetent crews. Early T-34s had transmission problems and during the invasion more broke down than were knocked out. This Model 1941 shows absolutely no battle damage. (*Scott Pick Collection*)

The T-34 first went into action at Grodno, Byelorussia, with the 6th Mechanised Corps on the day of the invasion. Its appearance caught the panzers by surprise, but there were not enough of them, nor did the crews know how to use them properly, as this pile-up demonstrates. Artillery or dive-bombers account for the mess, but the tanks should never have been so close together. (*Scott Pick Collection*)

Similarly, the KV-1 heavy tank had gone into production in February 1940 at Leningrad's Kirov works and was only available in limited numbers. This one came to rest in a massive crater. The discoloration on the front indicates that it caught fire. (*Scott Pick Collection*)

On the road to Moscow counter-attacks by the 6th and 11th Mechanised Corps and the 6th Cavalry Corps were smashed and the Byelorussian capital Minsk was duly encircled. This T-26 threw a track and had its hull pierced twice; its crew didn't stand a chance. A charred tanker lies half out the turret. (*Scott Pick Collection*)

German infantry plod past what looks to be a Model 1941 T-34. With the capture of Minsk on 28 June 1941 and the annihilation of Soviet forces in the area, the Germans claimed to have taken or knocked out almost 4,800 tanks. (*Scott Pick Collection*)

But the panzers did not have it all their own way, as this burnt-out Mk III testifies. The Red Army did all it could to throw back the Nazi Blitzkrieg but it was not enough. (*Author's Collection*)

Soviet counter-attacks on 26 June 1941 led to a huge tank battle involving some 2,000 tanks. They suffered appalling losses, such as this T-26; the infantry on the hull found no shelter from death. (*Scott Pick Collection*)

German soldiers examine a disabled SdKfz 232 armoured car (issued to the Panzerspäwagon squadrons), another victim of determined but ultimately futile Red Army resistance. (*Author's Collection*)

German troops marvel at the sheer size of this abandoned T-35. It may have looked impressive but with just 30mm of armour it was vulnerable to most anti-tank guns. In 1941 T-35s served with the 67th and 68th Tank Regiments, 34th Tank Division, attached to the 8th Mechanised Corps in the Kiev Special Military District. (*Scott Pick Collection*)

The majority of the T-35 heavy tanks were lost to mechanical failure and abandoned while serving with the 34th Tank Division during the summer battles in Ukraine. This particular example, after coming off the road, became stranded in the adjacent flooded field. It shows no visible signs of damage. (*Scott Pick Collection*)

The Soviet 30th Army lost almost half of its armour during early July trying unsuccessfully to fend off the 3rd Panzer Group. This burnt-out BA-10 is testimony to the fierce battles in which Stalin threw everything he had at Hitler's Blitzkrieg. (*Scott Pick Collection*)

Marshal Timoshenko, in a futile attempt to retake the Dnepr, launched 700 tanks at the Germans north of Orsha. This blood-splattered T-26 became the crews' tomb; once a tank was immobilised, escape was almost impossible. (*Scott Pick Collection*)

This grainy but atmospheric photo shows a smoking T-28 lying in a roadside ditch. At almost 10 years old, these medium tanks did not last long in action, with many breaking down, though some remained to help defend Leningrad and Moscow during the winter. (*Author's Collection*)

German soldiers with a KV-1. Ultimately Hitler's victory was due to his superior use of armour, speed, morale and better equipment. General Pavlov, Commander Western Army Group, who contributed to the Red Army's disastrous performance, was shot for his trouble. (*Scott Pick Collection*)

A German corporal and his mate tuck into their lunch in front of their Opel Blitz 3-ton lorry. Keeping the panzers resupplied over such vast distances was a full-time undertaking. Over 70,000 of these lorries were supplied to the Wehrmacht between 1937 and 1944. (*Author's Collection*)

A column of Opel Blitz lorries struggling through the mud. Russia's steppes turned into muddy quagmires during autumn and spring but were a frozen wasteland in winter. In Russia the appalling roads forced the Germans to convert conventional wheeled trucks into semi-tracks known as Maultiers. (*Author's Collection*)

Chapter Four

Zhukov's Moscow Miracle

On 16 September 1941 Field Marshal Fedor von Bock ordered the capture of Moscow under the codename Typhoon. Three panzer groups would spearhead the assault, with one of them being withdrawn from the attack on Leningrad. Although Hitler instructed the 3rd and 4th Panzer Groups to conduct two strikes opposite Moscow, following the Kiev victory von Bock added a third with Guderian's 2nd Panzer Group advancing from the southwest.

To resist almost 2 million German troops were 1.2 million Soviet troops of A. Yerëmenko's Bryansk Front, I.S. Konev's (having replaced Timoshenko in mid-September) Western Front and S.M. Budënny's new Reserve Front. Behind them the Vyazma Line was held by 84 rifle divisions, nine cavalry divisions, two motorised rifle divisions and a tank division, plus supporting services.

Hitler opened his attack against the Bryansk and South West Fronts on 30 September. Guderian's panzers quickly broke through the former and charged towards Orel. The 2nd Panzer Group pushed through towards Sevsk and Orel on Yerëmenko's left flank. Orel fell on 3 October, while General Joachim Lemelsen's XLVII Panzer Corps swung to the north to cut off Yerëmenko. However, Guderian's tanks suffered a reverse near Mtensk on 6 October at the hands of Soviet T-34s and his 4th Panzer Division suffered heavy casualties.

By 7 October the 3rd and 4th Panzer Groups had trapped the Soviet armies west of Vyazma in a vast pocket. Just a week later, on the 13th, resistance collapsed and a staggering 650,000 men laid down their arms, surrendering over 1,000 tanks and 4,000 pieces of artillery. This constituted some 45 divisions, almost half of Stalin's forces resisting Typhoon. The poor weather, combined with Hitler's demands that Tula to the northeast and Kursk to the south be captured, now slowed German progress.

Stalin chose this critical moment to reorganise his high command and the situation slipped from his grasp. The tried and tested Zhukov was summoned from Leningrad to organise the Mozhaisk Defence Line before Moscow. He found it far from complete, but bolstered it with six divisions, six armoured brigades and ten artillery regiments.

In reality, Army Group Centre was now far too stretched to constitute a real threat to Moscow; with the 2nd Panzer Group tasked to take Tula and envelop Moscow from the south, the 2nd Army striking from Kursk to Voronezh, 4th Army west of Moscow, 3rd and 4th Panzer Groups enveloping from the northwest and 9th Army instructed to help Army Group North, von Bock's front had expanded by a third. He wanted to attack Moscow by the shortest possible route, but found his original front had expanded from 400 to 600 miles.

During mid-October the only new and trained formation to reach the Soviet front was the Siberian 310th Motorised Division, though it arrived at Zvietkovo railway station without its vehicles. In early November troops from the Far East began to arrive in ever greater numbers, indeed Zhukov had doubled his strength by the time the German offensive commenced. The Far Eastern Front provided 17 divisions, eight tank brigades and one cavalry brigade, equipped with a total of 1,700 tanks and 1,500 aircraft.

Exhausted and lacking adequate winter clothing, the German armed forces were in a dire situation. Regardless of this, on 7 November Hitler issued orders for Typhoon to be resumed. This was based on the premise that the Red Army in front of Moscow was getting weaker not stronger. In reality, the West Front had received some 100,000 reinforcements with 300 tanks and 2,000 guns. Typhoon started again on the 15th and although the panzers got to within a few miles of Moscow, they were unable to make decisive breakthroughs either to the north or south.

In mid-November Stalin asked Zhukov if he could hold Moscow. The latter's response was 'yes' if he could have two additional armies and 200 tanks. He would be given the 1st Shock Army and the 10th Army but no tanks. The Siberians made their presence felt on 18 November when a division supported by an armoured brigade newly arrived from the Far East attacked the German 112th Infantry Division, which was guarding the 4th Panzer's push on Venev. The 112th, having already suffered 50 per cent frostbite casualties, was overrun by T-34 tanks. A week later German intelligence identified more fresh reserves from the Far East which had been thrown into the fighting, notably the 108th Tank Brigade and the 31st Cavalry and 299th Rifle Divisions.

On 2 December von Kluge's 4th Army was launched into the attack and advanced elements of the 258th Infantry Division penetrated Moscow's suburbs. Strong Soviet counter-attacks convinced von Kluge that he was not going to break through and that these advanced units should be withdrawn. This proved to be a prudent action as Zhukov threw 100 divisions into his general counter-offensive.

The German offensive was formally called off on 5 December; two days earlier some local withdrawals had already been sanctioned. The net result was that Zhukov held Moscow and von Bock lost his job to von Kluge. In January 1942 Konev opened a counter-attack supported by Rokossovsky's 16th Army and Vlasov's 20th Army. He pierced the enemy lines on the Volokolamsk Highway, while Zhukov attacked along the Mozhaisk Highway. However, German reinforcements from western Europe ensured things did not go according to plan for the Soviet commanders.

This culminated in a crisis at the junction of Zhukov's Western Front and the Bryansk Front. The Soviet offensive lasted until 20 April and Zhukov pushed forwards up to 155 miles, but in the process the Red Army suffered twice the losses of the Wehrmacht. In the north the offensive produced no results and in the south managed just 60 miles. In total the battle for Moscow lasted six months and cost Stalin 926,000 dead, not to mention wounded and missing. These colossal losses were greater than Britain and America lost in the whole of the Second World War. Zhukov, enjoying his first if flawed victory, recalled triumphantly, 'The Hitlerites lost on the battlefields of Moscow a grand total of over half a million men, 1,300 tanks, 2,500 guns, over 15,000 vehicles, and much other materiel.'

However you look at it, the summer of 1941 was a complete disaster for the Red Army. Its command structure and deployment of its tank divisions and mechanised corps proved a shambles. In the face of Hitler's panzers Soviet tanks such as the T-26 light tank and T-35 heavy tank, seen here slewed off the road, proved all but useless. Inexperienced and frightened tank crews died at their posts or abandoned their vehicles in terror. (*Scott Pick Collection*)

The death of a Soviet tanker becomes a tragic sideshow as German infantry come to gawp at his disabled T-26. The German army captured so many tanks that some were temporarily pressed into service for security duties behind the lines. (*Scott Pick Collection*)

Making good the colossal losses of July and August, such as this T-34/76B caught in a massive crater, became a priority for the Soviet high command. According to Marshal Zhukov, the first batch of new T-34s came off the Chelyabinsk Tractor Plant production line a month after the relocation of the Leningrad factory. The Sormovo shipyards in Gorky (Nizhniy Novogorod) on the Volga were also put to work producing T-34s, and these were employed during the battle of Moscow. Charged with defending the capital, Zhukov noted that they came just in time and played a conspicuous role in the fighting. (*Author's Collection*)

The burnt remains of a BA-10 armoured car and one of its crew. Rather late in the year three panzer groups were tasked with capturing Moscow, and Operation Typhoon opened on 30 September 1941. In the Bryansk and Vyazma pockets the Red Army lost over half a million men taken prisoner and over 1,000 tanks. Hitler's panzer divisions destroyed seven armies, including eleven Soviet tank brigades. (*Scott Pick Collection*)

By the time of the crucial battle for Moscow, 1,364 KV heavy tanks had been produced, although many had been captured or destroyed in the preceding months. Early models suffered clutch and transmission problems, and mobility was further compromised by the fact that the tank had to stop to change gear. This KV-1 threw a track and became stuck in the frozen mud with the onset of winter. (*Scott Pick Collection*)

Most KV-2 losses were due to breakdowns or lack of fuel. Although they were exceedingly well armoured, once the tracks had been shot off they were immobilised and the crew had little choice but to abandon their posts. (*Scott Pick Collection*)

Following the success of Operation Barbarossa, the panzer crews began to realise just how far from home they were. All eyes were now on the tank battles being fought to the west of Moscow. Hitler's generals knew that it was vital to take the city before the Red Army had an opportunity to recover from its crippling losses. (*Scott Pick Collection*)

Disastrously, in one swoop, Stalin lost almost half the forces opposing Typhoon but the Red Army rallied every available tank for the city's defence, including captured German armour such as this Panzer III and StuG III that were pressed into service. (*WH462*)

Judging by the paint splattered over the wheels and tracks, this Panzer III Ausf H command vehicle has just been whitewashed in some haste. Note the large frame antenna on the rear deck, the dummy 37mm gun and the turret bolted in place. (*Author's Collection*)

This KV-1 was lost just as the first snows began to fall. Judging by its dislodged turret, the ammunition exploded, instantly incinerating the crew. Note the large bolts securing the additional turret armour; this was a wartime upgrade that made the tank even heavier. Eventually the KV's contribution to the Soviet war effort was to provide the basis for the KV-85 and then the Joseph Stalin or IS heavy tank. (*Scott Pick Collection*)

KV-2 manufacture had been moved eastwards by October 1941 and some were employed unsuccessfully in the defensive winter battles for Moscow. They were little better than vulnerable mobile pillboxes. (*Author's Collection*)

A Panzer III pushing through a Russian town somewhere west of Moscow. The euphoria of the summer's victories was soon lost as General Guderian's 2nd Panzer Group suffered a bloody nose at Mtensk at the hands of the Soviet T-34, which began to redeem itself after its poor early performance. (*Scott Pick Collection*)

This BT-7, being looted for souvenirs or warm clothing, was destroyed during an engagement defending Moscow. The winter battles, though, did not repeat the wholesale disasters of the summer. (*Scott Pick Collection*)

A patrol of T-40 light tanks and supporting infantry. During a lull in Typhoon, under Zhukov's guidance Moscow's defences were bolstered by reinforcements from the Far East including 1,700 much-needed tanks. (A46)

By mid-November 1941 Stalin had directed Zhukov to conduct spoiling attacks south of the capital, resulting in more losses involving the 44th Cavalry Division. In contrast Siberian troops such as these anti-tank gunners supported by T-34s overran a German infantry division. (*Author's Collection*)

A Soviet cavalryman passing a knocked-out Panzer III. The Russian winter came as a terrible shock to Hitler's panzer forces, which were ill-prepared for the freezing conditions. General Guderian was furious at the slow provision of winter clothing. (*Author's Collection*)

Two destroyed T-26 tanks west of Moscow. The one in the foreground has been whitewashed for winter warfare. The mottling on the rear of the turret and the charred corpse on the engine grille show that the tank caught fire before the crew could bale out. (*Scott Pick Collection*)

The same tank from the rear. Clearly the supporting infantry were caught in the open by shell or machine-gun fire. (*Scott Pick Collection*)

A poor quality official Soviet photograph showing Soviet infantry in winter camouflage supported by a T-40 amphibious tank. Issued in February 1942, the original caption stated 'The Red Army's triumphant offensive . . . a magnificent picture from the advancing front line, illustrating the fine physique and high spirits of the heroic Soviet Soldier.' Propaganda aside, the Red Army's aggressive operations during the winter of 1941/42 showed that the weather would not inhibit its defence of the motherland. (*Author's Collection*)

Another Soviet photo of ski troops supported by a T-26 and a T-34. Zhukov's Moscow counter-offensive ran from early January to mid-April 1942 and successfully pushed the panzers back 150 miles. However, Stalin's forces suffered twice the casualties that Hitler's did, making it a costly and rather hollow triumph. (*Author's Collection*)

Chapter Five

Timoshenko's Kharkov Riposte

Making the most of Hitler's difficulties around Moscow, Stalin struck his positions south of Kharkov in Ukraine along the Northern Donets near Izyum on 18 January 1942. The German defences were overwhelmed and Soviet ski troops, infantry and cavalry poured into the Germans' rear areas, taking the rail junctions at Lozovaya and Barvenkovo. German mobility, though, meant that they were able to successfully contain the bridgehead, which stretched west from the Northern Donets towards the Donbas in the south and Kharkov to the north.

While Timoshenko and his South Western Front were preparing to liberate Kharkov, von Bock's Army Group South was aiming to destroy the Lozovaya pocket stretching southwest from Izyum beyond the Donets. General Friedrich Paulus to the north deployed his forces between Belgorod and Balakleya, while von Kleist to the south was at Pavlograd. Their intention was to cut off and destroy the Soviet salient, straighten the German line along the Donets and then launch their main offensive. Ironically Timoshenko obliged von Bock by effectively putting his neck in the noose.

Disastrously, two-thirds of the Soviet armour, along with General Kharitonov's 9th Army and General Gorodnyanski's 6th Army, moved into the salient ready to liberate Krasnograd southwest of Kharkov. This was to be followed by a push on Kharkov and Poltava way to the west. Their attack was to be supported by the Soviet 28th and 57th Armies north of Kharkov in the Volchansk bridgehead.

If von Bock had struck first he would have had to contend with nearly 600 Soviet tanks, but instead Timoshenko beat him to the post by attacking a week earlier on 12 May 1942. Those forces launched from Volchansk made little impression against Paulus' 14 divisions. In the south Romanian forces could not prevent the fall of Krasnograd and Kharkov seemed within Timoshenko's grasp. The Soviet 9th Army rolled on to Karlovka west of Kharkov. Worryingly, though, the Red Army was unable to widen the breach south of Izyum and Barvenkovo, which meant the pocket was getting bigger but not the breach.

If both the Soviet 6th and 9th Armies had struck towards Merefa south of Kharkov things might have gone differently, but with Kharitonov heading west on the 17th warning signs began to appear. This was the Soviets' first attempt at an armoured offensive on this scale and it had clearly not brought to battle the Germans' main combat strength, which was now identified as lying on their southern flank. Timoshenko prudently contacted Stalin to ask permission to slow down the offensive while he secured his flanks. In response Stalin was adamant that Kharkov was to be liberated.

With the noose tightening, Timoshenko dispatched his deputy General Kostenko to try to save the 6th and 9th Armies. When Paulus' panzers arrived at Balakleya on 23 May, linking up with those of von Kleist, the trap was snapped shut. Less than 25 per cent of the two Soviet armies got away, and all their heavy equipment was left littering the west bank of the Donets.

Officially the Soviets acknowledged 5,000 men killed, 70,000 missing and 300 tanks lost. The Germans claimed to have captured 240,000 men and taken or destroyed 1,200 tanks. Timoshenko only had 845 tanks in total, but the German figure may include all armoured fighting vehicles. It is doubtful whether any Soviet armour escaped the southern pocket, though the 28th Army may have saved a few in the north.

Stalin acknowledged Kharkov as a defeat, but not its magnitude – how could he after the humiliation of the previous summer? At the time the Red Army General Staff reported it had lost 266,927 men, 652 tanks and 4,924 guns and mortars. Of these, 13,556 dead lay in German-occupied soil while 46,314 sick and wounded had been successfully evacuated. The rest of this total had been captured.

The cost of the failed Kharkov offensive to the Red Army had been considerable, and while the tank ratio during 1942 had stood at 5:1 in their favour, it was now 10:1 against them, which did not bode well in light of the coming German summer offensive.

Stalin and his commanders had also learned the lesson that their pre-war mechanised corps were unwieldy and inflexible. Similarly the Barvenkovo operation had also taught them that their light mobile forces consisting of tank brigades and cavalry corps were simply not effective enough against German mechanised units or indeed, once behind enemy lines, against hastily assembled battle groups. The net result was that in the spring of 1942 the Red Army was ordered to create first mechanised and then tank corps that would be able to tackle the panzers on equal terms.

That summer von Bock launched the general German offensive with Operation Blue. This was to push east of Kursk against the Soviet South West Front to a line on the River Don between Livny and Rossosh, capturing Voronezh. Conducted by

German officers watch a burning Model 1940 T-34. Despite the Soviet Union's massive losses, it had 7,700 tanks by the beginning of 1942 and 20,600 by the following year. Stalin's relocated tank factories were churning out 2,000 a month, rising to almost 3,000 by the end of 1943. (*Author's Collection*)

General von Weichs' 2nd Army and Hoth's 4th Panzer Army, the plan was to create left flank protection for the 'Donets Corridor' along which Paulus' 6th Army could advance to Stalingrad.

On 28 June the Germans struck from the Kursk area in the direction of Voronezh, attacking the Bryansk Front's 13th and 40th Armies. From the start the Soviets were outgunned and outnumbered. In the face of Hoth's panzers the Soviet 40th Army disintegrated within 48 hours and the 13th Army was obliged to withdraw northwards. On the 30th the German 6th Army attacked Ostrogozhsk, penetrating the defences of the 21st and 28th Armies (the latter having been mauled at Volchansk in May) and both were caught in the open by German firepower. Two days later the Germans struck below Kharkov, with Kleist leading the 1st Panzer Army over the Donets. Once again Stalin's armoured forces were in disarray.

Another relic of the previous summer's bitter tank battles: a battered and flipped BT-5 light tank. As the holes clearly testify, its thin armour proved singularly ill suited to coping with German anti-tank guns. While both the BT and T-26 remained in service in the Soviet Far East, the BT was phased out on the Eastern Front through a simple process of attrition. (*Scott Pick Collection*)

The spring thaw in 1942 played havoc with both sides' military vehicles. The steel road wheels on this T-34/76B were not ideal for such soft conditions, though the wide tracks helped. Dirt roads soon turned into seas of mud, hampering troop concentrations and the movement of vital supplies. (*Scott Pick Collection*)

The T-70 light tank, armed with an improved 45mm gun, went into production in March 1942, with 8,226 having been built by the end of the following year. Although the hull armour was given better angles of protection and the driver had an armoured visor, modifications to the Panzer III and IV armament and armour easily cancelled out such improvements. The Red Army deployed 261 T-70s at Kursk, where they proved unsuitable for an offensive combat role. (*Author's Collection*)

The first Soviet tank armies, the 3rd and the 5th, appeared in the spring of 1942. Designed as breakthrough forces, they were blooded at Kharkov, on the Bryansk and Voronezh Fronts and on the approaches to Stalingrad. (*L32*)

The Panzer IV first appeared in 1937 with the L/24 gun; the up-gunned version (seen here under inspection) with the long barrel L/43 gun entered service in the spring of 1942. By the summer there were 170 examples on the Eastern Front, rising to 840 the following summer. Those Panzer IVs lost during the invasion were replaced by April 1942, but there was no increase in overall numbers. In terms of production Germany could not compete with Russia: in November 1942 the Germans managed 100 Panzer IVs compared to 1,000 Soviet T-34s. (*Author's Collection*)

Soviet tankers go for a drive in a captured StuG III Ausf E (distinguishable from earlier models by the armoured side pannier). Production of this model stopped in March 1942. Such reuse was restricted by the availability of spares and ammunition. (*Author's Collection*)

The arrival in 1942 of the Sturmgeschütz III Ausf F fitted with the StuK40 L/43 or L/48 long barrel 75mm gun gave the front-line troops an effective anti-tank weapon that could easily defeat the KV-1 and T-34. It was to remain in production right up until the end of the war. In December 1942 Panzer III assembly was entirely turned over to the StuG III assault gun. (*Author's Collection*)

The rather top-heavy-looking 76.2mm Pak 36 mounted on the Panzer II Ausf D chassis provided a useful stopgap self-propelled anti-tank gun. Some 200 were built during 1942 and 1943, with most of them ending up on the Eastern Front with the panzerjäger units. (*WH832*)

In the New Year, while Hitler and his generals were distracted around Moscow, Stalin also struck south of Kharkov in Ukraine with two of his new-style Soviet tank corps. Marshal Timoshenko's South Western Front was ordered to drive the Nazis out of Ukraine but inadvertently got caught in a trap. (*BA28*)

A sightseeing German officer in front of Kharkov's main square. The city was a vital communications and logistical hub for Hitler's operations in Ukraine. To both sides it represented a strategic and political goal that could not be ignored, and as a result it was the scene of four major engagements. (*Scott Pick Collection*)

In the spring of 1942 Timoshenko attempted the Red Army's first major armoured counter-offensive, but it was ill-planned and his armour was not up to the job, and it ended with disastrous results. Only four of the fourteen tank brigades committed were combat tested; likewise only one of the two supporting tank corps had any experience. (*Scott Pick Collection*)

Two-thirds of Timoshenko's tanks moved into the exposed Barvenkovo-Lozovaya salient south-east of Kharkov and counter-attacked on 12 May 1942, but in the process simply drove themselves deeper into the German noose. These abandoned BT-7s seem to have run into each other. (*Scott Pick Collection*)

The Soviet 9th Army with two of the inexperienced tank brigades reached Karlovka, making the pocket deeper without increasing the breach. This photo shows the smashed and smoking remains of a KV-1 and T-34. (*Scott Pick Collection*)

A Red Army 122mm Model 1938 howitzer surrounded by its dead crew. This gun was used widely on the Eastern Front. Attempts to marry the Model 1938 with the T-34 chassis under the designation SU-122 were not entirely successful. (*Scott Pick Collection*)

By 23 May 1942 two whole Soviet armies were trapped by the panzers, losing 845 tanks. All attempts to escape the ever-contracting pocket failed. This T-34 has been blown over on to its turret and seems to be a source of much interest to these German troops. (*Scott Pick Collection*)

With the Red Army's armour smashed in Ukraine, Hitler's panzers now enjoyed a 10:1 superiority. However, the LT-38 or PzKpfw 38(t) seen here was deemed no longer suitable for front-line use and production was given over to Marder self-propelled guns from April 1942. (WH492)

The now famous Tiger PzKpfw VI Ausf E went into production in mid-1942 and the first unit to be equipped with it fought in the Leningrad area in August that year. Although nothing at the time could penetrate the Tiger's thick armour, the sheer weight of Soviet firepower resulted in some being captured. (WH881)

A German soldier cleaning the windscreen of his Mercedes-Benz LG63. Safeguarding such supply and transport vehicles from Soviet partisans tied up considerable resources. Note the chains on the rear wheels – they must have been expecting bad weather! (*Author's Collection*)

A whitewashed Panzer III Ausf L. Judging by the supplies on the back, it has just redeployed. This variant was in production from mid- to late 1942 and was used to replace combat losses and equip the SS panzergrenadier divisions. (*Author's Collection*)

Chapter Six

Disaster at Stalingrad

The newly created Stalingrad Front absorbed the battered South Western Front, reinforced with the newly formed 1st and 4th Tank Armies. By 22 July the Stalingrad Front numbered 38 divisions, with 16 divisions deployed in the main defensive zone. It was their job to fend off the 18 divisions of the German 6th Army.

The Germans attacked Stalingrad's first defensive line on 17 August 1942, with General Gustav von Wietersheim's XIV Panzer Corps breaking through five days later to reach the Volga north of the city. His panzer corps split the Stalingrad defence near Vertyachi and the Soviet 62nd Army was cut off from the Stalingrad Front and was transferred to Yerëmenko. German bombers pounded Stalingrad to rubble and the following day the panzer corps attacked towards the Tractor Works but was cut off for several days by a Soviet counter-attack. To the south of the city the South Eastern Front was forced to withdraw on first the outer and then the inner defences.

The 4th Panzer Army's two panzer corps reached the second line of defence by the end of the month and the third by mid-September. The battle then turned into bitter urban warfare that dragged on until 18 November, by which time the Germans had reached the limit of their offensive. From that point on they were on the defensive.

By early November 1942 Hitler's strength on the Eastern Front, according to Soviet intelligence, totalled about 6.2 million men organised into 266 divisions equipped with 5,080 tanks and assault guns. Soviet industrial muscle had ensured that by this stage Stalin's massive losses of 1941 had been made good. Soviet manpower stood at about 6.6 million men equipped with 7,350 tanks. On top of this the Soviet high command had considerable reserves. It was time for them to strike back.

The main attack for Stalin's Operation Uranus was to be launched over 100 miles west of Stalingrad and would cut southeastwards. At 6.30am on 19 November 3,500 Russian guns opened up on the Romanian 3rd Army's positions. Trenches and bunkers were smashed as the barrage ranged in. Men staggered about in a deafened daze as their inadequate defences collapsed in the face of the concerted onslaught.

Then came the Soviets' dreaded T-34s clanking across the snow-draped landscape. Most of the Romanian defenders took fright and fled.

The Soviets broke through in two places. This was achieved by General Romaneko's 5th Tank Army launching itself from the bridgehead southwest of Serafimovich and General I.M. Chistyakov's 21st Army attacking from the Kletskaya bridgehead. The Romanian 1st Tank Division and Romanian 7th Cavalry Division were thrown into the fight to halt the 5th Tank Army, but the tank division was easily brushed aside.

The 26th Tank Corps' advance guard seized a bridge over the Don on 26 November. The Germans mistook the attack for an exercise using captured Russian tanks and the armour rumbled unopposed over the bridge. Kalach lay a little over a mile away, but the German defenders were not so easily overwhelmed until Soviet reinforcements arrived. Far to the southeast the Romanian 4th Army suffered a similar fate, just 24 hours after the South Western and Don Fronts had opened the offensive.

In an attempt to stem the advance on Kalach, the 16th and 24th Panzer Divisions foolishly got in the way. By 4pm on 23 November the Soviets were in the vicinity of Sovetsky to the east of Kalach. It was only a matter of time before a link-up was effected, trapping the Germans deployed between the Don and the Volga. The next stage was to destroy the Axis forces trapped in the Kessel ('Cauldron'), as the Stalingrad pocket became known.

Stalin also launched Operation Mars on 25 November 1942, designed to destroy the German forces in the Rzhev salient. This involved the Kalinin Front supported by the 1st and 3rd Mechanised Corps, as well as the Western Front supported by the 5th, 6th and 8th Tank Corps and the 2nd Guards Cavalry Corps.

Unlike Uranus, this offensive was not destined to be a resounding success. The intended victims were not ill-prepared and ill-equipped Romanians, but tough German divisions that were well dug in. Furthermore, help was at hand: at Rzhev the German 9th Army had the 1st and 9th Panzer and Grossdeutschland and 14th Panzergrenadier Divisions in reserve, while the 19th and 20th Panzer Divisions were also within reach; Western Front was faced by the 5th Panzer Division.

On the 25th the two mechanised corps broke through the German defences north and south of Beyli, and only bad weather and determined German resistance finally brought them to a halt. To the north the 39th Army hit the Germans northeast of Rzhev, while to the west it struggled to cut the Rzhev–Olenio railway. During December German reserves succeeded in destroying the 1st Mechanised Corps and the 6th Rifle Corps. The 3rd Mechanised Corps was driven back and contained. The Western Front alone lost 42,000 dead and 1,655 tanks by 14 December.

Von Manstein's highly capable and experienced 11th Army HQ was formed into the new Army Group Don to coordinate Operation Winter Storm: the relief of 6th Army. This mission was assigned to the rump of 4th Panzer Army remaining outside Stalingrad, now grandly named Armeegruppe Hoth under General Herman Hoth.

It was intended that Hoth would make a single concerted thrust using General Friedrich Kirchner's LVII Panzer Corps, comprising the 6th and 23rd Panzer Divisions, later bolstered by the 17th Panzer Division. Looking at the map, both von Manstein and Hoth realised that the shortest route to Stalingrad was from Nizhne Chirskaya, but this was not the best path for success. In the region lay the 5th Tank and 5th Shock Armies of Lieutenant N.F. Vatutin's South West Front, the key players in the success of Operation Uranus.

With 230 tanks of 6th and 23rd Panzer Divisions, plus air support from the Luftwaffe, the operation commenced on 12 December. Initially it made some headway but waiting in reserve were the Soviets' 4th and 13th Mechanised Corps. The Soviets quickly realised what was going on and committed not only the 4th Cavalry Corps but also the 7th Tank Corps and the 2nd Guards Army belonging to the South-West Front. In the face of such resistance the panzers could make no further progress.

Having smashed the Romanians so effectively, Stalin set about crushing the other Axis armies. Operation Saturn, following the encirclement of Stalingrad, smashed the Italian 8th Army to create a larger pocket of trapped Axis forces. On 16 December Soviet tanks crashed into the Italian army and two days later it was surrounded.

A Panzer III Ausf J made ready for winter warfare. During the summer of 1942 there were 1,100 Mk IIIs armed with the 50mm gun serving with the panzer divisions at the front. (*Author's Collection*)

A Marder II also whitewashed for the winter. This type consisted of the Panzer II chassis and a Pak 40 75mm anti-tank gun, and production ran from June 1942 to June 1943, when Panzer II facilities were turned over to the Wespe 105mm self-propelled gun. Nonetheless, with over 650 built it remained in service until the end of the war. (*WHPanzer*)

At 6.30am on 19 November 1942 some 3,500 Soviet guns heralded Stalin's Stalingrad counter-offensive. Behind this massive bombardment came the tried and tested T-34. Those troops in its path had good reason to fear it. (*B84*)

Obsolete Hungarian, Italian and Romanian anti-tank guns were incapable of stopping the T-34/76. A half-hearted counter-attack by a Romanian tank division was simply swept away in the chaos of their disintegrating armies. (*Author's Collection*)

The Don provided little protection for the ill-equipped German forces and their allies against Stalin's Operation Uranus, launched in the winter of 1942 some 100 miles west of the ruined city of Stalingrad. (*Scott Pick Collection*)

German defences in the Stalingrad area were ill-prepared to withstand a major Soviet offensive. This entrenched 88mm gun, though, would have provided a nasty surprise if it withstood the Red Army's preliminary bombardment. (*Scott Pick Collection*)

German infantry awaiting the inevitable appearance of Soviet infantry and their supporting T-34s. Dug-in troops often found the pace of such attacks quite unnerving. The T-34 was well suited to the Russian weather; its wide tracks and low ground pressure gave it good traction and speed. (*Scott Pick Collection*)

By the winter of 1942 nearly all the German army's Czech 38(t) light tanks had been worn out, and their chassis given over to a highly successful range of self-propelled guns and tank destroyers. (*WH491*)

These SdKfz 222 crews were wrapped up against the bitter cold of the Russian winter. Armed with a 20mm gun, almost 1,000 of these light armoured cars were built and they remained in service on the Eastern Front until the end of the war. (*Author's Collection*)

A German officer dressed for the weather with the remains of a Pak 40 anti-tank gun. (*Scott Pick Collection*)

The winter of 1942, like the previous winter, proved to be an endurance test for the tank crews of both sides. Vehicles had to be kept operational regardless of the freezing weather. The crew of this Panzer IV are having a spring clean during a lull in the fighting. Lice were always a problem. (*Author's Collection*)

German infantry taking cover from Soviet armour behind what appears to be a 75mm Infanterie Geschütz support weapon. (*Scott Pick Collection*)

Some 270,000 German and other Axis troops were trapped in the Stalingrad pocket after the Romanian army collapsed along the Don and Volga rivers. By this stage the city was in ruins and its remaining population starving. (*Author's Collection*)

At the same time three Soviet tank corps struck the Rzhev salient. However, on this occasion Hitler's armour was much better prepared and the Red Army lost 1,655 tanks in the face of stiff German resistance. Remarkably Stalin was able to shrug off such losses thanks to his tank factories. (*K9*)

Winter conditions were far from ideal for the frozen gun crews, but at least the tanks presented good targets exposed on the snow-draped landscape. (*Scott Pick Collection*)

A frozen leFH 18 105mm gun crew laying down supporting fire – which would last only as long as the ammunition did. (*Scott Pick Collection*)

Localised and desperate counter-attacks by the panzers were insufficient to prevent Soviet armour bursting through on both sides of Stalingrad and snapping the trap closed on the German 6th Army. (*Scott Pick Collection*)

Field Marshal von Manstein himself oversaw Operation Winterstorm, a futile effort to bludgeon a way through to those forces encircled at Stalingrad using three panzer divisions. It ended in failure. (*Scott Pick Collection*)

A Red Army anti-tank gunner armed with a PTRD 1941 anti-tank rifle stands proudly in front of an Italian L6/40 light tank he had knocked out northwest of Stalingrad. (*Author's Collection*)

Cannibalised panzer hulks abandoned near Kotelnikovo southwest of Stalingrad. This photo was taken by a Soviet photographer for the Ministry of Information in December 1942 or January 1943. (*Author's Collection*)

Abandoned German equipment, including this Panzer IV, lay at the mercy of Soviet souvenir hunters. Stalingrad was one of the first major setbacks that the German army suffered on the Eastern Front, and the troops found it increasingly difficult to bounce back from the disaster. In terms of deploying its armour, the Red Army had drawn on the important lessons gained at Kharkov. (*BA51*)

Chapter Seven

Manstein's Kharkov Comeback

In early 1943 Stalin was pressing forwards to the Oskol, Donets and Don rivers. As well as thrusting southwest to Kharkov, he also opted to punch west towards Kursk in order to exploit the 200-mile gap torn between von Kluge's Army Group Centre and Army Group Don (shortly to be renamed South). On 1 February he launched Operation Star, employing the Voronezh Front supported by the 3rd Tank Army. In the meantime the South West Front swung southwest to take Mariupol on the Sea of Azov, cutting Army Group Don's communications with Army Group A in the Caucasus.

By 5 February, three days after the last pocket in Stalingrad surrendered, General Rybalko's 3rd Tank Army had reached the Donets east of Kharkov. The Voronezh Front liberated Volchansk, Belgorod, Oboyan and Kursk and by the 11th was on the outskirts of Kharkov itself. The South West Front was soon deep in Army Group Don's rear. Stalin had every prospect of trapping the 1st and 4th Panzer Armies and Armygruppe Hollidt against the Sea of Azov. Only after the personal intervention of von Kluge and von Manstein did Hitler agree to allow a withdrawal to the River Mius.

At Kharkov the newly arrived I SS Panzer Corps was pushed back. Paul Hausser, its commander, fearing Kharkov could become another Stalingrad, disobeyed Hitler and evacuated the city on 15 February. In the meantime the main Soviet threat was a salient thrusting towards Dnepropetrovsk. While the Germans held the Red Army west of Kharkov, von Manstein orchestrated a counter-attack on 19 February, using I SS Panzer Corps striking south from Krasnograd southwest of Kharkov towards Pavlograd. Three days later Hoth's 4th Panzer Army linked up with the SS.

On the southern side of the salient, the 1st Panzer Army's XL Panzer Corps joined the attack, defeating Group Popov near Krasnoarmeysk. The Soviets saw this operation as a means of covering the 1st Panzer Army and Armygruppe Hollidt's withdrawal from the Mius to the Dnepr. In response the South West Front was instructed to hold the Germans on the Mius. However, von Manstein's success at

Pavlograd enabled him to push forwards some 150 miles, thereby threatening the recently liberated Kharkov. Indeed, he unhinged the junction of the Soviet South West and Voronezh Fronts and the Soviet advances were stopped. The Red Army lost 23,000 men dead and 9,000 captured, as well 615 tanks knocked out.

Rybalko's 3rd Tank Army swung south to take on the I SS Panzer Corps on 24 February. The SS withdrew to lure Rybalko into a trap, which resulted in the Red Army losing another 9,000 dead and 61 tanks. The 3rd Tank Army had to fight its way from the Kharkov area and Stalin agreed to a withdrawal to the Donets. Rybalko's defeat left Kharkov open to von Manstein once more.

Following the Soviet victory at Stalingrad, Stavka planned an offensive to capitalise on the successes of the Bryansk and Voronezh Fronts along the Voronezh–Kursk axis and support the South Western Front's push through the Donbas to the Dnepr and the Sea of Azov. This was scheduled to begin on 12 February when the Western and Bryansk Fronts were to surround the Germans' Orel salient. The two fronts supported by the Central Front were to clear the Bryansk region and gain bridgeheads over the Desna between the 17th and 25th. Afterwards the Kalinin and Western Fronts were to take Smolensk and help destroy Army Group Centre in the Rzhev–Vyazma salient.

However, in the Donbas von Manstein threw back the South Western Front and the Western Front failed in the Zhizdra area. Also Rokossovsky's offensive was delayed to 25 February; his Don Front (renamed the Central Front) was to be spearheaded by the 2nd Tank Army. Within two weeks it had gained Sevsk, while the 2nd Guards Cavalry Corps reached Trubchevsk and Novgorod-Severskii. However, south of Orel progress was slow and on the left flank the Soviets were tied up trying to turn the German 2nd Army's left flank.

Rokossovsky was denied victory by the delayed arrival from Stalingrad of the 21st Army (subsequently diverted to Oboyan to counter von Manstein's move on Belgorod), bad weather and by von Manstein's counter-stroke that smashed the Voronezh Front south of Kharkov. The fighting continued until 23 March, but Rokossovsky's troops gave up Sevsk to take up positions that would become the northern and central faces of the Kursk salient.

Field Marshal von Manstein launched the second phase of his powerful counter-offensive on 6 March and by the 14th was back in control of Kharkov. The Germans claimed to have killed another 50,000 men and captured 19,594 as well as destroying 1,140 tanks. The recapture of Kharkov was a bitter affair. In just over two months the SS Panzer Corps alone sustained over 11,000 casualties, the 1st SS Panzer Division losing 4,500 of these during the recapture of Kharkov.

Stalin had already decided to dispatch reinforcements, including the 1st Tank Army, to the Belgorod area, but they were not in place quickly enough to save the city, which fell to von Manstein on the 18th. Nonetheless, two armies were able to move into blocking positions northeast of Belgorod and this thwarted von Manstein's attempt on Kursk. Zhukov managed to stabilise matters by 26 March and the spring thaw brought the mobile warfare to a halt.

The fall of Kharkov and Belgorod marked the conclusion of the Army Group's second counter-blow, as the increasing muddiness of the ground did not permit further operations. While Manstein had achieved a remarkable reversal of fortunes at Kharkov, he lost the opportunity to move against the Soviets' Kursk salient to shorten the German front. This scheme had to be abandoned, as Army Group Centre was unable to cooperate. As a result the salient continued to mark a troublesome dent in the German line.

The Germans were sufficiently impressed by the T-34 to warrant reusing it. In the case of the 2nd SS Panzer Division, Das Reich, it captured T-34s straight off the factory line in Kharkov. One battalion within the division's 2nd Panzer Regiment was equipped entirely with them. (*Author's Collection*)

Luftwaffe officers examine a captured British Matilda III CS armed with a 3in howitzer. Britain supplied Stalin with Churchill, Matilda and Valentine tanks, while America provided the M3 Lee and M4 Sherman. By 1943 20 per cent of Soviet tank brigades were using Lend-lease armour and over 10 per cent were entirely equipped with them. During 1941 and 1942 Britain and the Commonwealth supplied Russia with 3,270 tanks and America supplied another 7,000 from then until the end of the war. (*Author's Collection*)

The T-26 was obsolete even in 1940; while its 45mm gun could destroy all German armoured vehicles except the Panzer IV, it suffered from problems common among Russian tanks: mechanical unreliability and thin armour. By 1943 Stalin's tank factories were working hard to replace the remaining T-26 and BT-7 tanks with the proven T-34. (*Author's Collection*)

After the T-34 the SU-76 light self-propelled gun was the most widely produced Soviet armoured vehicle during the Second World War. Using a T-70 chassis mounting a 76.2mm anti-tank gun, it appeared in 1943. It was later replaced by the SU-85 tank destroyer as an anti-tank platform and switched to an infantry support role. (K14)

The crews hated the SU-76 because of its open fighting compartment and thin armour, which gained it the nickname *Suka* ('Bitch'). This photo shows just how exposed they were – both to the elements and to enemy fire. (*Author's Collection*)

The Panzer III was kept in production until August 1943 with the Ausf M armed with a 50mm gun and the Ausf N with a short 75mm gun (155 of the latter were deployed at the battle of Kursk). This looks to be an earlier J model. (*Scott Pick Collection*)

A blurry shot of an advancing Grille 150mm self-propelled gun. This was another German stopgap using the Czech 38(t) chassis. Only 90 of this particular variant were produced in early 1943, some of which saw action on the Eastern Front. (*Author's Collection*)

By 11 February 1943 the Red Army had fought its way to the gates of Ukraine's second city Kharkov. This poor quality Soviet propaganda shot shows a group of infantry armed with submachine guns dislodging the Germans from an inhabited district on the outskirts of Kharkov. (*Author's Collection*)

A Panzer III armed with a 50mm gun and its support vehicles are dwarfed by the vast expanse of Kharkov's Red Square. General Hausser, fearing another Stalingrad, evacuated his forces four days after the Soviet attack commenced. Retreating ensured that his panzers regained the initiative. (*Scott Pick Collection*)

Soviet T-34/76Ds liberated Kharkov on 15 February 1943; because the Germans had withdrawn in such haste, the Red Square remained largely undamaged. The reoccupation lasted just a month. (K78)

A new Model 1943 T-34, having caught a Tiger by surprise on a raised causeway, moves in for a closer look. The Tiger proved to be far from invincible. (BA18)

A Red Army anti-aircraft battery installed in Kharkov's Red Square to guard against Luftwaffe reprisals in mid-February 1943. (*Author's Collection*)

A hulled-down StuG III Ausf G, identifiable by the cupola and the slanted superstructure. Later Ausf Gs from November 1943 were fitted with the *Topfblende* or pot (often erroneously called *Saukopf* or 'pig's head') gun mantlet without coaxial mount. However, the original box mantlet also continued to be produced. The G variant was the final, and by far the most common, of the series with almost 8,000 manufactured. (*WH190*)

Barely pausing for breath, von Manstein counter-attacked at Kharkov on 19 February 1943 using the tough II SS Panzer Corps, which linked up with the 4th Panzer Army at Pavlograd. The second phase of his counter-stroke was launched on 6 March and within a week he was back in possession of Kharkov, much to the dismay of the population. (*Scott Pick Collection*)

German infantry examining the charred remains of T-34 tank crews, who escaped their blazing tanks only to be mown down in the snow by machine-gun fire. In the face of Manstein's counter-attack, the Red Army lost 32,000 men and 615 tanks. (*Scott Pick Collection*)

By the summer of 1943 the T-34/76 had overcome its initial teething problems and was well battle proven, causing an acceleration in German tank designs to try to counter it. Ironically, the German Panther, about to make its debut at Kursk, was to suffer the same problems. (K5)

The 85mm M39 anti-aircraft gun provided the solution to up-gunning the T-34. It was one of the best gun designs to come out of Russia and its dual anti-aircraft/anti-tank capability made it an ideal candidate to equip the T-34 and SU-85. The initial T-34/85-I that appeared in 1943 was basically an up-gunned T-34 using a turret originally designed for the KV-85 and armed with an 85mm D-5T gun. (*Author's Collection*)

Chapter Eight

Clash of the Titans – Kursk

Stalin's operations had left him in possession of the vast salient around Kursk, flanked by enemy forces centred in the south on Kharkov and in the north on Orel. Belatedly Hitler's intention was to snip off the salient, employing all available means. Capitalising on his spring victory on the German right, Field Marshal von Manstein's Army Group South, spearheaded by Hoth's 4th Panzer Army and General Werner Kempf's Armeegruppe Kempf, was to attack northwards from Belgorod and Kharkov.

For the battle of Kursk Hitler gathered the greatest force ever assembled on such a small front. Barbarossa had flung 3,332 panzers at the Soviet Union along a 930-mile front; for Citadel Hitler squeezed 2,700 tanks along just 60 miles. Some 63 per cent of all battleworthy armour on the Eastern Front was assigned to von Kluge and von Manstein. While this sounded impressive, with 1,850 front-line panzers, 200 obsolete panzers and 533 assault guns divided among 16 panzer and panzergrenadier divisions and three assault gun brigades, the units were seriously under strength. By 1943 a panzer division had a theoretical strength of up to 200 panzers and 15,600 men. In reality the average strength was just 73 tanks. However, the II SS Panzer Corps' divisions averaged 166 panzers and assault guns.

Hitler's generals, though, were hoping that the newly deployed armour would help to counter the Red Army's growing strength. It offered the opportunity to destroy Soviet tanks at arm's length and stop them closing in, which would prevent the panzers from being overwhelmed by superior numbers. Indeed, for the first time since Barbarossa Hitler was fielding tanks and self-propelled guns that had a distinctive qualitative edge. He was placing great faith in his menagerie of tanks and fighting vehicles named after wild beasts, notably the Tiger, Panther, Elefant (Ferdinand), Rhinoceros, Bison and Grizzly Bear. It was anticipated that these would tear great holes in the ranks of the Soviet tank corps.

Crucially, though, these vehicles were not yet available in decisive numbers. There were fewer than 90 Ferdinands, about 200 Panthers and about 100 Tigers; over 1,000 older Panzer III and IVs remained the backbone of the panzer forces. Also making their debut were the Hummel, the Nashorn or Hornisse, and the Marder III or Wespe. Again numbers were a problem: all three types had only gone into production in early 1943, with about 100 of each type ready for the summer. To help smash Soviet fortifications there were 66 newly built Brummbar comprising a short 150mm howitzer mounted on a Panzer IV chassis.

Stalin was not only well prepared for Hitler's massed panzers but he was ready to switch over to his own offensive once they had been stopped. The Soviet defences around Kursk were formidable: by June 300,000 civilians had dug a series of eight in-depth defences stretching back almost 110 miles. Using brute strength, picks and shovels they carved out almost 3,100 miles of trenches. Just to be on the safe side, the reserve Steppe Front had dug its own defences to protect the eastern bank of the Don.

The fields of wheat and corn ripening in the summer sun concealed another deadly secret that would tear machines and men apart with ease. Soviet sappers toiled to sow over 40,000 mines across the length and breadth of the salient. In the killing grounds between the strongpoints they meticulously concealed about 2,400 anti-tank and a further 2,700 anti-personnel mines per mile. Initially, as the panzers and supporting infantry blundered through these, they would be deluged by fire from howitzers and heavy mortars supported by anti-aircraft guns.

Once through the minefields the panzers would encounter 'pakfronts' consisting of batches of anti-tank guns supported by anti-tank rifles, machine guns and mortars. The plan was that along expected lines of attack the panzers would meet clusters of guns whose job it was to funnel them into yet more minefields. There was little doubting the quite extraordinary volume of fire that the Central and Voronezh Fronts could call upon – at their disposal were 6,000 anti-tank guns, 20,000 guns and mortars and 920 Katyusha rocket batteries.

Operation Citadel commenced on 4 July 1943, making little headway before being checked. Hausser's II SS Panzer Corps struck towards Bykovka with 365 tanks and 195 assault guns. The SS took the town, while other units cut the Oboyan–Belgorod road, only to be obstructed by the Soviet 96th Tank Brigade. Similarly a penetration was made on the right flank but the panzers could get no further. The strength of the Soviet defensive positions stopped the Germans breaking through north of Belgorod, which was to cause Hoth problems.

Model advanced just 6 miles before being halted in front of Olkhovatka and Ponyri, losing 25,000 men, 200 panzers and 200 aircraft in the process. Manstein's forces managed 25 miles, losing 10,000 men and 350 panzers. Stavka was not slow to react and during the night of 8/9 July they hastened to get the 5th Tank Army with 630 tanks and self-propelled guns and the 5th Guards Army to the Prokhorovka region.

Within six days Citadel had run out of steam; for the first time a German panzer offensive had been stopped before achieving a breakthrough. By the 13th von Manstein claimed those forces facing him had lost 24,000 men captured as well as

1,800 tanks. Also that day von Manstein and von Kluge were summoned to East Prussia, where Hitler informed them that Citadel must be called off as the Allies had landed in Sicily, thereby threatening Italy.

At this point Zhukov unleashed his massive counter-offensive, sweeping back the panzers' hard-won gains and pushing them out of their Orel and Kharkov salients to the north and south of the Kursk bulge. Operation Kutuzov ran from 12 July to 18 August, working to destroy the Germans' Orel bulge, which overlapped with Operation Polkovodets from 3–23 August against the southern sector of the bulge. This pushed the Germans back, liberating both Belgorod and Kharkov. The success of this operation meant that Hitler's forces in Ukraine were obliged to withdraw behind the Dnepr and paved the way for the liberation of Kiev.

The battle for Kursk lasted 50 days and according to Soviet sources cost Hitler 30 divisions, including seven panzer divisions. Zhukov recorded their casualties as half a million men and 1,500 tanks. But the Soviet victory came at a terrible price. Casualties for the three Soviet Fronts totalled 177,847 men and 1,614 tanks and self-propelled guns: five times those of the Wehrmacht. However, from this point on Hitler was on the defensive on the whole Eastern Front.

By mid-1943 Soviet tank crews had much to smile about, having recovered from the disasters of 1941 and 1942. During Barbarossa, Hitler's meagre panzer force had thrown around 3,300 tanks at a 930-mile front; for Citadel at Kursk a 60-mile front was attacked by 2,700 tanks. Nevertheless, the 5th Tank Army was more than capable of bearing the brunt of the powerful II SS Panzer Corps. (AO120)

Too much was expected of the new Panzer V Ausf D Panther, which Hitler rushed off the production line to take part in the Kursk offensive. Drawing on the T-34, it combined armament, armour and mobility; equipped with the 75mm L/70 (an improved version of that equipping the Panzer IV), it could knock out Soviet tanks almost as easily as the Tiger. Although the Panther's frontal armour was on a par with the Tiger's, its side armour was little better than that of the Panzer IV. Early models proved mechanically unreliable, in part due to being sent into combat much too quickly. (*Author's Collection*)

Panther deployment was considered a vital element of Operation Citadel and the offensive was delayed as a result of their mechanical problems, with the eventual start date being just six days after the last Panther was delivered. The T-34's 76.2mm gun could penetrate the Panther's side armour at up to 1,000m, but could only penetrate the glacis armour at 300m and could not overcome the turret frontal armour at all. An improved armoured-piercing round was not introduced until October 1943. While its debut at Kursk was inauspicious, the Panthers claimed 267 enemy tanks destroyed. By 10 August 1943 just 43 of the original 250 Panthers were still in operation. (*K191*)

The Tiger was armed with an 88mm gun that could outshoot the T-34 at a range of 1,500 metres, whereas the latter had to close to 500 metres. Fortunately for the Red Army, fewer than 60 Tigers were available, but nonetheless they proved a great success. The T-34, with a maximum of 70mm frontal armour, was already vulnerable, even at 1,000 metres, to the Panzer IV Ausf F2's 75mm Kwk40 L/43 gun (which could penetrate 87mm of armour), and the subsequent Panzer IV Ausf G and H were both armed with the Kwk40 L/48. (*Author's Collection*)

The highly successful Sturmgeschütz 40 Ausf G. For the Kursk offensive the Germans massed 533 assault guns; while some were integrated with the panzer divisions, most operated in independent brigades. (*Author's Collection*)

To supplement the StuG IIIs armed with 75mm guns, the 105mm Sturmhabitze 42 appeared in March 1943. This one is based on the Ausf G hull. At the start of the battle for Kursk Army Groups Centre and South had 68 StuH42s providing very welcome fire support. (*Author's Collection*)

Limited numbers of the Elefant/ Ferdinand Sturmgeschütz were issued to two Panzerjager units in the spring of 1943, and 90 were available at Kursk. Armed with the powerful 88mm Pak 43/2 anti-tank gun, the type utilised the chassis of the rejected Porsche design for the Tiger tank. The II SS Panzer Corps was equipped with the Ferdinand, but it lacked secondary armament and was very vulnerable to close-range attack. (*Author's Collection*)

The Nashorn/Hornisse, which united the 88mm Pak 43/1 L/71 gun with the Panzer Mk IV chassis, was also a capable tank killer for the German tank-hunting battalions, though essentially it was a defensive weapon. It first saw action on the Eastern Front in the summer of 1943. It proved to be one of the most effective anti-tank guns deployed during the war. The ability to engage the enemy at long distances negated the disadvantages of light armour and a high profile, and the weapon was well suited to the open Russian steppe. (*WH334*)

The Hummel 150mm gun on the Panzer IV chassis (seen here) and Wespe 105mm self-propelled gun utilising the Panzer II chassis both first saw major action at Kursk in 1943. The Wespe proved so successful that Hitler ordered all Panzer II production to be switched to this self-propelled gun. (*Author's Collection*)

The Junkers Ju 87 G-2 was nicknamed *Panzernacker* ('tank cracker') because of its 37mm tank-busting guns. Their efforts were greatly appreciated by the panzer crews, although at Kursk it proved to be a sitting duck for Soviet fighters. (*Scott Pick Collection*)

The Focke-Wulf Fw 190 was a superb fighter and ground-attack aircraft. Using fragmentation bombs in support of the SS Panzer Corps, they played a key role in helping achieve the initial penetration of Soviet defences. (*Author's Collection*)

A panzer column with infantry support advancing across the flat Russian steppe – ideal tank country. At Kursk Hitler's intention was to throw every last panzer into a bid to nip off the vast Soviet salient and then crush those troops trapped in the pocket. Little did he appreciate that Stalin was preparing for a much wider envelopment and that his panzers were advancing into a deadly trap. (*Scott Pick Collection*)

A column of German StuG IIIs moving up for the attack. Hitler must have been hoping that Kursk would see a repeat of the fighting for the Barvenkovo salient and Kharkov, where the Red Army had come so badly unstuck. Perhaps he naively thought the victories around Leningrad and in the Crimea could also be relived. (*Author's Collection*)

T-34s break cover from their camouflaged position; it was at times like this that they were at risk of attack by the Luftwaffe. The lead tank is a Model 1941, followed by a Model 1942. Soviet tank design was largely moribund at this point, the priority being simply to churn out as many tanks as possible. This meant that the Model 1943 that had superseded the 1940, 1941 and 1942 models was not greatly different. (*K6*)

Only 200 Soviet tanks at Kursk were heavies and the battle marked the swansong of the much maligned KV-1. The Panthers and Tigers picked many of them off at long range. (*Scott Pick Collection*)

In response to the Tiger Stalin had up his sleeve the SU-152. A redesign of the KV-1 chassis, it was armed with a massive 152mm howitzer that could be used in an anti-tank role. Only 12 were available for Kursk, but they claimed 12 Tigers and 7 Elefants destroyed, and as a result the SU-152 gained a reputation as a 'Beast' killer. (*BA211*)

Late on 11 July the Soviet 5th Tank Army dispatched two tank brigades to prevent Prokhorovka falling into enemy hands. A major tank battle occurred there the following day. (*Scott Pick Collection*)

A column of Model 1943 and 1941 T-34/76s en route to the battle at Prokhorovka. Many were probably destroyed in the fighting. (K17)

The 7.62mm divisional field gun proved its worth during the summer of 1943. (AO153)

The Heinkel He III medium bomber was deployed extensively at Kursk in support of the panzers. However, by mid-1943, like the Stuka, it was vulnerable to enemy fighters. (Author's Collection)

The Panzer III was still in service at this stage of the war, though the newer models were armed with the short 75mm gun, previously fitted on StuG IIIs and Panzer IVs. Outgunned and under-armoured, these Panzer IIIs armed with the 50mm gun were no match for the Soviet steamroller. It looks as if they were caught by artillery or air attack. (K184)

The Shturmovik ground-attack aircraft was greatly feared by the panzer crews. (Scott Pick Collection)

General K.K. Rokossovsky offers his thoughts on this captured Ferdinand. The fact that its armour withstood three direct hits must have impressed the Soviets, but once it had thrown a track it was useless, its crew left to the mercy of the Soviet infantry. (K180)

An overturned British Matilda II; in Red Army service, the type was used in an infantry support role. Britain sent 1,084 Matildas to the Soviet Union, where it was the second most common British tank after the Valentine. The Matilda II was the only British tank to serve throughout the whole of the Second World War. (WH553)

Chapter Nine

Stalin's Steamroller – Bagration

In late 1943 Stalin sought to liberate Ukraine west of the Dnepr, thereby undermining Hitler's exposed flank in Byelorussia to the north. The 1st Ukrainian Front included two tank armies, and these forces were soon in Kiev driving back the 4th Panzer Army. Then in the New Year 370 tanks moved to successfully trap those German units in the Korsun–Shevchenovsky salient. This victory crushed the last of Hitler's offensive strength in Ukraine. In late March 1944 more German troops were also caught in the Kamenets–Podolsk pocket as Soviet armour sought to crush the 1st and 4th Panzer Armies. The following month German troops were swiftly ejected from the Crimea. Also from January to March the Red Army fought to lift the siege of Leningrad.

It is almost impossible to imagine the noise of over 4,000 revving engines. This was the number of tanks that Stalin massed for Operation Bagration; his version of D-Day, it was launched in the summer of 1944 and was designed to liberate Byelorussia. Throughout the first half of the year his tank factories had worked flat out to make good his losses and then some. By the time of the offensive he had 11,600 armoured fighting vehicles on the Eastern Front.

Stalin commenced battle with 2,715 tanks and 1,355 assault guns, about six times the number deployed by Hitler's Army Group Centre. Predictably, nothing could withstand such brute force. To make matters worse, the loss of armoured units to northern Ukraine and France meant that the army group was largely an infantry force. Critically, it only had 553 of the 4,740 tanks and assault guns on the Eastern Front and most of these were in fact assault guns. The bulk of the armour, 40 panzers (including 29 Tiger Is) and 246 StuG IIIs, was deployed with General von Tippelskirch's 4th Army defending the city of Orsha.

On top of this Army Group Centre had no real reserves except for a weak panzer division, the remains of a panzergrenadier division and an infantry division. Overall, the balance sheet favoured Stalin, with 3:1 in manpower, 10:1 in tanks and self-propelled artillery and 8:1 in guns and mortars. The correlation of forces was such that Hitler's forces would be overwhelmed if they did not conduct a swift fighting withdrawal.

General Reinhardt's 3rd Panzer Army held the northern wing. Despite being nominally a panzer army, this formation had no panzer or panzergrenadier divisions. On the right of the 3rd Panzer Army lay the 4th Army south of Mogilev, running northwards between Mogilev and Orsha. It could muster just two panzergrenadier divisions. General Jordan's 9th Army holding the Bobruisk area running roughly south to north had a single panzer division at Bobruisk.

Following a massive artillery barrage and air attacks Stalin's steamroller, spearheaded by T-34s, struck on 23 June. The deluge of hot metal pouring onto their positions stunned the defenders and whole units were simply swept away. By mid-afternoon Army Group Centre had informed the German high command that in the face of Stalin's pincer movement the situation around Vitebsk looked precarious and Reinhardt's 3rd Panzer Army did not have the ability to restore the situation.

By early afternoon on the 25th the 1st Tank Corps had reached the Dvina and taken a damaged bridge. Soviet tanks overwhelmed Tippelskirch's XXXIX Panzer Corps and the 3rd Panzer and 9th Armies fell apart. General Jordan's 9th Army received permission to commit the 20th Panzer Division to try to stem the onslaught of T-34s. The division could muster just 71 Panzer IVs. At that moment the 65th Army broke through on the southern approaches to Bobruisk and the 1st Guards Tank Corps moved to exploit the breach. Perhaps panicking, Jordan ordered the 20th Panzer Division to retrace its tracks and head south, bumping into the Soviets near Slobodka south of Bobruisk.

Now not only was Bobruisk under threat but also those German divisions still east of the Berezina river. By the 26th the tanks of the 20th Panzer Division had been driven back to the city with the Soviet 9th Tank Corps bearing down on them from the east and the Soviet 1st Guards Tank Corps advancing from the south. The 1st Guards Tank Corps cut the roads from Bobruisk to the north and northwest on the night of 26/27 June.

Two pockets were created in the Bobruisk area, trapping nearly 40,000 men. Attempts by von Lützow's XXXV Corps to break out to the north spearheaded by 150 panzers and self-propelled guns were smashed on the evening of the 27th. The 20th Panzer Division led the breakout northwest along the western bank of the Berezina, with the rearguard instructed to hold on until 2am on the 29th. The panzers and panzergrenadiers soon found themselves under attack by T-34s and fighter-bombers.

By 30 June the first phase of Bagration was over; according to the Soviets, they had killed some 132,000 Germans as well as capturing or destroying 940 tanks. The German 4th Army found itself being squeezed by seven tank, motorised and cavalry corps. The Byelorussian capital Minsk was liberated on the evening of 3 July and the people danced in the streets.

The near-total annihilation of Army Group Centre in the space of just under two weeks cost Hitler overall casualties of 670,000, and only about 20,000 troops escaped. In addition, he lost (according to Soviet figures) 2,000 panzers and 57,000 other vehicles. Stalin's losses were 176,000 killed and wounded, plus about 8,000 missing, and 2,957 tanks. The work of Stalin's Bagration steamroller was complete; his armour now looked ready to liberate the rest of Ukraine and strike into southern Poland. During 20–29 August the Red Army thrust into eastern Romania with the Jassy–Kishinev offensive. The denuded Army Group South in Ukraine had only three armoured units and was quickly overwhelmed.

The Soviets introduced new up-gunned tanks in 1944 that finally gave them parity with the best of the German heavy and medium panzers. The previous autumn a turret similar to that on the KV-85 was mounted on the T-34 chassis, creating the T-34/85. The Model 1943 turret displayed a unique style of bolted collar and was equipped with the shorter D-5T 85mm gun, capable of penetrating the frontal armour of the German Tiger at 1,000 metres, although accuracy remained a problem. This interim model also featured a rounded front-hull join, rounded front fenders and no turret fillet. Approximately 800 Model 1943 T-34/85s were produced at Gorkiy early in 1944. (A048)

The T-34/85 was deployed in conjunction with the SU-85, an 85mm self-propelled gun mounted on the T-34 chassis. This heavily armoured assault gun appeared in the battles in Ukraine in 1944 but was subsequently replaced by the SU-100, mounting a more powerful 100mm M1944 field gun. (AO45)

The Russians introduced only one new tank in this period, the IS (also known as JS) or Iosef Stalin, although in truth this was not an entirely new design but rather a redesigned KV. Although classed as a heavy tank, it was roughly the same weight as the Panther medium tank. The IS-1 or IS-85 (after the calibre of its gun) was developed alongside the KV-85 and entered service in September 1943. (AO42)

The IS was initially equipped with an 85mm, then a 100mm and finally a 122mm gun, enabling Soviet tank crews to engage any German tank type at extremely long ranges. The IS-2 went into production in late 1943; 102 were made in that year, but the following year Soviet factories churned out some 2,250. The up-gunned IS-2 first saw action in Ukraine in early 1944, claiming 41 Tigers and Elefants for the loss of only eight tanks. (B21)

The mighty ISU-152 also appeared in late 1943 as a successor to the SU-152, which gained the nickname 'beast killer'. Armed with a powerful 152mm howitzer, they were grouped into independent heavy assault gun regiments and brigades, which were attached to the tank corps in a support role. For Operation Bagration the Red Army had 295 ISU-152s and ISU-122s. (AO44)

This display of confidence by Soviet tankers and infantry was well founded by this stage of the war. In January 1944 the 6th Tank Army was formed with about 600 tanks and self-propelled guns, 500 guns and mortars and 30,000 men. Stalin's six tank armies had nearly 40 armoured corps. (K22)

The Tiger did not have the desired effect on the Eastern Front. While it could knock out any Soviet tank before the latter got within range, it was slow and expensive to build. Also, once disabled, it was difficult to recover (only six Tiger recovery tanks were ever built). The fierce fighting in January 1944, in which many Tigers were lost, established the new front lines ready for Stalin's massive summer offensive codenamed Bagration. (WH916)

Although the Panzer IV was the German workhorse on the Eastern Front, the earlier Ausf D, E and F armed with the short 75mm gun were phased out through attrition in early 1944. The panzer divisions were equipped with the newer F2, G and H variants, although they were in danger of being outclassed by some of the newer Soviet armour. (BA24)

In February 1944 the StuG III, StuH42 and StuG IV began to appear with the cast *Saukopf* (sow's head) gun mantlet seen here. By the summer Army Group Centre's panzer force consisted almost entirely of assault guns. (*Author's Collection*)

The Ausf G was the third and final series of the Panther, which went into production in March 1944 and was deployed to the Eastern Front. (*Author's Collection*)

The PzKpfw VI Ausf B, better known as the Tiger II, was issued to German combat units in the summer of 1944, five months after production started. Although it was capable of dealing with Soviet armour with ease, like the Tiger I it was never produced in sufficient numbers to stem the flood of enemy tanks. (*AO36*)

By early 1944, despite massive losses sustained at Kursk and in Ukraine, the Red Army was still able to field 5,357 tanks and self-propelled guns thanks to Soviet industry. For the Byelorussia offensive in June Stalin committed the bulk of his armoured forces, including five tank armies, plus ten separate tank and mechanised corps. (K10)

T-34/76Ds moving up for the attack with infantry tank riders; by June 1944 this was the most common tank in service with the Red Army. The previous year over 15,500 T-34/76s had been built, but production was now prioritised for the T-34/85. (K25)

The open-topped SU-76M was deployed for Bagration. It was intended to provide the infantry with direct artillery fire support, but it also had a secondary anti-tank role. While the gun was more than adequate for such duties, the crew protection was not. (B26)

After slicing through Army Group Centre's defences, the 2nd Guards Tank Corps equipped with the new T-34/85 was the first unit into Minsk when it was liberated on 3 July 1944. (AO47)

In the summer of 1944 Stalin's Operation Bagration overwhelmed Hitler's Army Group Centre in Byelorussia. The loss in men and materiel was enormous. Here the Russians have gathered a selection of captured anti-tank weapons, including two types of Pak 43 88mm guns. Note also the hand-held Panzerfaust lying on the ground to the right. (*Author's Collection*)

A disabled PzKpfw IV in front of a Soviet M3 Stuart light tank supplied by America under Lend-lease. Throughout 1944 Hitler lost 2,643 Panzer IVs on the Eastern Front. The previous year he had suffered losses of 2,352 Panzer IVs with some divisions down to as few as 12 tanks; such losses were increasingly difficult to replace. The no-frills Panzer IV Ausf J which appeared in 1944 was the final production model and was greatly simplified to speed construction. The manual turret traverse was not greatly liked by the crews. Production ran until March 1945, by which time nearly 3,000 of this type had been produced. (*Author's Collection*)

T-34/85s of the 4th Tank Corps on the streets of the Romanian capital Bucharest on 31 August 1944. Hitler's Axis allies on the Eastern Front proved to be a house of cards; outgunned by the Red Army, there was little Hungary and Romania could do to stem the tide. (*Author's Collection*)

The Panzer IV/70 tank destroyer also appeared on the Eastern Front in 1944 after it went into production that August; it was used to supplement the StuG IV and Jagdpanzer IV. (*Author's Collection*)

The crews of these T-34/85s take a break in what are clearly blizzard conditions. Even during the winter of 1944 there was little respite from the fighting. Stalin and his generals were determined that the panzers should not be permitted time to recuperate. However, Hitler was still able to launch two major counter-offensives. (*Author's Collection*)

Chapter Ten

T-34s on the Oder

Hitler's intelligence was well informed of Stalin's intentions in early 1945. It was calculated that his attack would begin on 12 January with an advantage of 11:1 in infantry and 7:1 in tanks. An evaluation of Stalin's total strength gave him a superiority of approximately 15:1 on the ground and 20:1 in the air. Stalin launched his Vistula–Oder offensive as predicted, which took the Red Army from the Vistula in Poland to the Oder east of Berlin.

The 2 million men of Zhukov's 1st Byelorussian and Konev's 1st Ukrainian Fronts, supported by 4,529 tanks and 2,513 assault guns, simply overpowered the 400,000 troops of Army Group A, supported by 1,150 panzers. After 23 days they had torn open a breach 625 miles wide by 375 miles deep, and swept across the Oder. The 1st Byelorussian Front secured a bridgehead at Kustrin just 35 miles from Berlin.

By the end of the first week of February in Silesia the Germans' Oder defence had collapsed and the Red Army was beyond the left flank of the Upper Silesian front. On the night of 12 February Soviet troops came together in the Tinz–Domslau area encircling Breslau. The key point in this battle occurred on the 13th, when the 19th Panzer Division in the Kostomloty area held open the autobahn to enable two infantry divisions to escape. That night the 7th Guards Tank Corps succeeded in sealing off the rest of the garrison. By 15 February Soviet forces had surrounded Breslau as the 3rd Guards Tank Army closed the gap to the west.

Striking from Greiffenberg, the 8th Panzer Division made a surprise attack three days later against the southern wing of the Soviets advancing from Löwenburg to Lauban. Although they slowed them, on the 28th Lauban fell to the 3rd Guards Tank Army, allowing them to prepare to move on Görlitz and Dresden. The Germans counter-attacked with elements of the 8th, 16th and 17th Panzer Divisions, knocking out 230 Soviet tanks and halting the advance.

It was not until early March that the Germans attempted to relieve Breslau, gathering seven divisions including four panzer divisions in the Gorlitz area. On the 3rd they attacked the weak 3rd Guards Tank Army, but after fierce fighting the attack was halted with both sides suffering heavy casualties.

Stalin sought to clear the rest of Silesia with the Upper Silesian offensive conducted from 15 to 31 March 1945. Konev launched his main assault with the 4th Tank Army piercing the German lines west of Oppeln and heading southwards for Neustadt. Southeast of Oppeln Soviet forces also broke through the German defences, swinging westwards to link up with the 4th Tank Army. By the 22nd the Soviets had crushed the Oppeln 'cauldron', claiming to have killed 15,000 Germans and captured a further 15,000.

In Hungary German troops were trapped in Budapest and the IV SS Panzer Corps was diverted from Warsaw in late December 1944 to rescue them. They did have some opportunity of breaking through as initially they had 70 per cent more troops and 140 per cent more armour than the Soviet 4th Guards Army holding the outer ring. Operation Konrad I was launched on 1 January 1945 and saw the SS strike from the north of the city; attacks were also conducted to the west.

Konrad III, the last part of the operation, commenced on 17 January with IV SS Panzer Corps and III Panzer Corps attacking from the south with the aim of trapping ten Soviet divisions. Again this failed. During the second counter-attack 100 panzers supported by two regiments of motorised infantry tried to punch through the Soviet 5th Guards Airborne Division. Eighteen panzers made it through, only to run into a Soviet anti-tank regiment, which accounted for half the tanks.

Following the loss of Budapest, Hitler, desperate to hold back Stalin in Hungary, ordered ten panzer and five infantry divisions to launch a counter-offensive between Lake Balaton and Lake Velencze, dubbed Operation Spring Awakening. He had a 2:1 superiority in tanks, and the Soviet forces in Hungary were weak in armour, which meant that anti-tank guns would be their main defence against the 900 panzers and assault guns thrown at them. The Soviet anti-tank gunners were particularly contemptuous of the Panzer IV, which they considered obsolete. However, the area chosen for the attack between the River Danube and the northern end of Lake Balaton was criss-crossed by canals and ditches and was unsuitable for mobile armoured warfare.

On the morning of 6 March 1945, after a 30-minute artillery bombardment supported by air attacks, the Germans launched a furious three-pronged attack, with the 6th SS Panzer Army striking in a southeasterly direction between Lakes Velencze and Balaton; the 2nd Panzer Army thrusting eastwards in the direction of Kaposvar; and Army Group E attacking northeast from the right bank of the Davra with the aim of linking up with the 6th SS Panzer Army.

Two days after Spring Awakening opened, the 2nd SS Panzer Division reinforced the offensive with 250 tanks, followed by the 9th SS the next day. The Red Army found itself under attack by almost 600 panzers. Nevertheless, Hitler's forces were rapidly running out of time and resources – his factories had been all but wrecked by the repeated attentions of the Allies' bombers. In a final desperate push for the

Danube, Spring Awakening's last reserves, the 6th Panzer Division with 200 tanks and self-propelled guns, were committed on 14 March. They managed to force their way to the Soviet rear defence lines, but got no further.

On 16 March Stalin launched his own counter-offensive west of Budapest, hitting General Balck's 6th Army and the Hungarian 3rd Army north of Lake Velencze. Motorised infantry rolled through a breach, which 12th SS Panzer Division tried to block, and the Red Army swept southwest towards Balaton. The Soviets sought to encircle the 6th SS Panzer Army and 6th Army.

The inadequately equipped Hungarians on II SS Panzer Corps' left flank defected with inevitable results. The skeletal Hungarian 3rd Army withdrew westwards and under pressure the 1st SS Panzer Division gave ground, exposing Balck's flank. Six days later the 6th SS Panzer Army was trapped south of Szekesfehervar and barely escaped.

A commissar hitches a ride on a T-34. Although the Red Army did not differentiate between the variants, the Model 1946 entered service during 1945 and saw front-line action in the closing days of the 'Great Patriotic War'. It could be distinguished from the Model 1945 by its fuller lower turret sides and the new configuration of ventilator domes. (*Author's Collection*)

The Model 1945 T-34/85 (which confusingly entered service during 1944) differed from the Model 1944 in that it featured a larger cupola, which extended close to the port edge of the turret, requiring a tiny lip underneath on the turret side. (B19)

Soviet infantry attacking with tank support provided by T-34/76Ds. By early 1945 the Soviet tide was relentless. Hitler's exhausted Army Group A had just 1,150 panzers to halt Stalin's massive Vistula–Oder offensive, which committed 4,329 tanks and 2,513 assault guns to the battle. (A046)

While the panzers could knock out the IS-2, they had no real answer to its 122mm armament, which easily outgunned them. When Stalin's Oder–Vistula offensive opened on 12 January 1945, German intelligence estimated that Soviet forces had a 3:1 numerical superiority; in fact they had a 5:1 advantage. (AO41)

Abandoned Wespe and Hummel self-propelled guns. By the time the Soviet 3rd Guards and 4th Tank Armies' assault began, the 4th Panzer Army had lost up to two-thirds of its artillery and a quarter of its troops thanks to Soviet field guns and air attack. (RGAKFD via author)

The two panzer corps of the 4th Panzer Army were quickly overwhelmed and forced to withdraw. German Tigers lay abandoned in the mud; once immobilised, there was no way to retrieve them. The corrugating on the turret is Zimmerit anti-mine coating, which was applied as a paste. (BA52)

An ISU self-propelled gun on a pontoon ferry. The 2nd Guards Tank and 5th Shock Armies reached the Oder almost unopposed and crossed over, taking Kienitz as early as 31 January 1945. Once over the Oder the only other major defensive barrier before Berlin was the Seelow Heights. (B89)

Panzergrenadiers and a supporting assault gun taking a break from the fighting. At Breslau the 19th Panzer Division enjoyed limited local success when it manage to extricate two infantry divisions; the city, though, was promptly surrounded by Soviet armoured formations. (WH968)

For ten days the tanks and StuGs of the 8th Panzer Division struggled to defend the city of Lauban. This assault gun is clearly overloaded with panzergrenadiers anxious to hitch a lift. (*WH335*)

Panzergrenadiers wearing heavy-duty winter parkas moving up for a counter-attack in SdKfz 251 armoured personnel carriers. In early March the panzers attempted to cut their way through to Breslau but without success. Although Hitler's panzer forces were ebbing away, the defenders held out until the end of the war. (*WH327*)

A StuG III abandoned in a Soviet vehicle park with various other captured armoured fighting vehicles. Once Stalin's tank factories were in full swing, the Red Army had little need to recycle enemy tanks. The Ausf G was the last production series of the StuG, first rolling off the assembly line in December 1942; by March 1945 some 7,720 had been produced. (*RGAKFD via author*)

Another wrecked StuG pictured in 1945 by a Soviet combat photographer. In Hungary Hitler refused to abandon Budapest to the Red Army. Operation Konrad tried to relieve the garrison in the New Year of 1945 using SS panzer divisions. When this attempt failed, two more futile attempts were made. (*RGAKFD via author*)

To counter Red Army advances in Hungary, Hitler launched a massive counter-attack in March 1945. Despite a 2:1 tank superiority, this failed to have the desired effect and the Soviet counter-offensive swept his panzer forces away. Stalin was now the master of Blitzkrieg, though in his hands it was a blunt instrument. (AO146)

Reportedly 287 Panzer IVs were lost on the Eastern Front during January 1945. It is estimated that the Red Army accounted for 6,153 Panzer IVs or about 75 per cent of all Panzer IV losses during the war. (WH441)

Chapter Eleven

Seelow and the Last Tank Battles

By early 1945 Hitler's panzer forces were on their last legs, but remained determined to put up one last fight against Stalin's coming assault on Berlin. Hitler as ever remained obsessed with launching counter-attacks using formations that were little more than flags on a map. Zhukov arrived in Moscow on 29 March to discuss their plans. His intelligence indicated that Hitler had four armies in the region with no fewer than 90 divisions, remarkably including 14 panzer and motorised divisions. However, from the very beginning the battle was a one-sided affair. In total the Red Army fielded 2½ million troops, equipped with some 6,250 tanks. Zhukov was able to hurl almost a million men of the 1st Belorussian Front against Berlin's outer defences anchored on the Seelow Heights.

In his path lay about 100,000 exhausted troops of General Theodor Busse's 9th Army, which formed part of Army Group Vistula. He defended the front that encompassed the Seelow Heights. In total the 9th Army had 14 division with 512 panzers, 344 artillery pieces and 300 anti-aircraft guns. Further south the front was held by the exhausted 4th Panzer Army, tasked with fending off the vengeful 1st Ukrainian Front.

General Weidling, commanding the LVI Panzer Corps, observed the sheer weight of Zhukov's attack: 'On 16 April, in the first hours of the offensive, the Russians broke through on the right flank of the 101st Army Corps on the sector of Division Berlin, thereby threatening the left flank of the LVI Panzer Corps.'

Coordination of the Seelow assault, though, proved chaotic, signals traffic overwhelmed the decoders and Zhukov, desperate for results, continually meddled. He needed to take the heights that morning to allow the breakout to encircle Berlin, otherwise Konev would get the credit. He soon discovered he had completely underestimated the strength of the defences.

General Mikhail Katukov, commander of the Soviet 1st Guards Tank Army, was ordered to bludgeon his way through the Germans on the heights. However, throwing the 1st and 2nd Guards Tank Armies into the fight did not immediately have the desired effect. The original plan was that they would exploit the breakthrough, not achieve it. Due to the swampy ground the tanks had to use the roads that were already packed with infantry. This created major traffic jams and provided the German anti-tank gunners with prime targets. Predictably German artillery caught the Soviet tanks in the open. Even when the tanks did reach the escarpment they found the gradient too steep to climb and were knocked out in great numbers. The 65th Guards Tank Brigade, Katukov's vanguard, found the going tough and the defenders desperately clung on to their positions. Southeast of Seelow the Soviet armour ran into Tigers of the 502nd SS Heavy Panzer Battalion.

Despite the stubborn resistance, Katukov gained a foothold on the heights. The 9th Army weathered three days of preliminary attacks and then spent 24 hours enduring the full force of Zhukov's assault. They knocked out over 150 Soviet tanks but it was not enough. In just three days the 1st Belorussian Front smashed through the final defences of the Seelow Heights, leaving little in the way of effective defence between the Soviets and Berlin. The Germans lost some 11,000 killed, while the Red Army suffered 30,000 dead. All that remained to defend Berlin itself were about 45,000 troops.

The Red Army assaulted Berlin itself on 21 April 1945. It threw 6,250 tanks into a massive assault to encircle the beleaguered Nazi city; the Germans in stark contrast had just 650 panzers to defend it. According to Soviet figures, there were just 200 panzers facing the British and American forces in the West, while there were 1,500 protecting Berlin; this estimate was wildly inaccurate. Crouching behind their T-34s, ISs and self-propelled guns, the Soviets battled their way along Berlin's streets as the final battle was played out.

Units of the 3rd Assault, 2nd Guards Tank and 47th Armies were committed to the attacks on the outskirts of Berlin and four days later the city was assaulted from the southeast by General Berzarin's 5th Shock Army and General Katukov's 1st Guards Tank Army. Along the northern bank of the Teltow Canal facing Rybalko's 3rd Tank Army were some 15,000 men with 130 tanks.

During the desperate fighting German troops succeeded in breaking through the Soviet encirclement twice, though on both occasions they were stopped. In the Beelitz area 30,000 men from the German army almost reached General Wenck's 12th Army, which had been sent from the Western Front to help Berlin. Konev claimed that only 4,000 men got through.

Hitler's remaining panzers tried to flee on 1 May. The Soviets, suspecting they were carrying fleeing Nazi officials, knocked them out 10 miles northwest of the shattered city the following day. That same day the German garrison surrendered. The Red Army claimed it lost 2,156 tanks and self-propelled guns taking Berlin and that it captured over 1,500 panzers and assault guns. During the course of the entire war the Red Army lost a staggering 96,500 tanks and self-propelled guns.

Stalin's very last armoured assault of the war was the Prague Offensive, conducted after Berlin had been overwhelmed. Fought from 6 to 11 May it culminated in the liberation of the Czech capital. Army Group Centre, which had been at the very heart of Operation Barbarossa and Hitler's dream of capturing Moscow, fought to the very last. It did not surrender until nine days after the Red Army had captured Berlin and three whole days after Victory in Europe Day. The last of Hitler's panzers lay disabled on the streets of Prague.

By early 1945 Stalin's Blitzkrieg had bludgeoned its way across Eastern Europe, capturing Danzig, Konigsberg, Warsaw, Budapest and Vienna. Hitler's armoured counter-attacks did little to forestall the inevitable in the face of Stalin's armoured might, spearheaded by these T-34/85s. (BA3)

The IS-2 had an improved hull with contour castings and proved to be one of the most powerful tanks to go into service with any army during the Second World War. Nonetheless it did not have it all its own way: in at least one recorded instance in March 1945 a single Panther accounted for four of them – clearly they must have been a highly experienced crew with nerves of steel. (RGAKFD via author)

This late production StuG IIII Ausf G is all but buried in the mud and would have presented a difficult target to destroy. By late March 1945 Stalin was poised to assault Berlin itself. The city's eastern defences were anchored on the Seelow Heights, defended by 512 panzers and assault guns – the equivalent of about five panzer divisions. (*RGAKFD via author*)

Concrete dragon's teeth east of Berlin. Such man-made obstacles did little to impede the Red Army's tanks and the defences on the Seelow Heights were far from complete. (*RGAKFD via author*)

The 2nd Guards Tank Army's tanks stormed into the shattered suburbs of Berlin on 21 April 1945. Crouching behind its IS-2s (as seen here), T-34 tanks and self-propelled guns, the Red Army fought its way along Berlin's broad avenues, streets and roads and through its parkland. (*RGAKFD via author*)

A Lend-lease Sherman rumbles through Berlin's suburbs. After the war Stalin chose not to acknowledge the role played by British and American tanks in his war effort. (*RGAKFD via author*)

Built-up areas were hardly an ideal combat environment for tanks, but Stalin cared little for such niceties. Here a T-34 takes up position in one of Berlin's parks; the city's defenders were well armed with panzerfausts, which meant the tankers had to constantly sweep the street with machine-gun fire. (*RGAKFD via author*)

A Soviet 76.2mm anti-tank gun helps take out the last of the panzers on the streets of Berlin. Half a dozen Tiger IIs or King Tigers were involved in these final bitter tank battles defending the government quarter. (*RGAKFD via author*)

The final resting place for a Panzer V Panther turret; note the lucky (or extremely accurate) shot that pierced the gun mantlet. This would have killed the crew instantly and detonated the tank's ammunition. Hitler's last 20 operational panzers were knocked out 10 miles northwest of Berlin on 1 May 1945. (*RGAKFD via author*)

With the Berlin garrison subdued, a T-34/85 crew take in the views beneath the city's famous Brandenburg gate. (*RGAKFD via author*)

A column of IS-2 Stalin tanks photographed on 8 May 1945 in the woods west of Berlin. Note the French prisoners of war heading home. (*Author's Collection*)

The Red Army claimed the battle for Berlin cost it 2,156 tanks and assault guns, showing the ferocity of the German army's last-ditch defence. Hitler's panzer forces were no more and the Soviets captured over 1,500 tanks and assault guns. (BA55)

The very last tank battles were fought on the streets of Prague in the closing days of the war. The 2nd SS Panzer Division covered the German evacuation as the Red Army liberated the city on 9 May 1945. This burnt-out Czech-built Jagdpanzer 38(t) was one of the very last victims of the armoured warfare on the Eastern Front. (*Author's Collection*)

Crowded with Soviet troops and cheering Czech civilians, a T-34/85 rolls through the streets of Prague, giving Stalin his last victory of the war. (*Author's Collection*)

The shattered remains of a StuG assault gun on the streets of Prague. (*Author's Collection*)

A Red Army column in Prague, including another T-34 covered in Soviet infantry. (*Author's Collection*)

The war's end. With the final tank battles over, the crews of a T-34/85 and a Lend-lease Sherman admire the mountains in Czechoslovakia. Army Group Centre (which had been in the forefront of Operation Barbarossa), with two nominal panzer armies, surrendered on 11 May 1945. (*Author's Collection*)

DATE

A new generation of Cold War warriors is born. The IS-3 with its frying-pan turret, which appeared in the Allied Victory parade in Berlin in 1945, heralded the new shape of Soviet armour to come. Reportedly a few saw action during the final stages of the battle for Berlin. (*RA31*)